Linda Meissner, Tacoma 1971

Linda Meissner and Kathryn Kuhlman

Linda speaks at Greenlake

Linda's graduation, Montezuma High School

What people are saying about The Voice

In this unique, historical book Linda Meissner takes you back in time to the 60s and 70s with such vivid autobiographical stories that you literally feel part of the extraordinary events of those days. This book is definitely a "must read" for everyone who dares to dream of an upcoming revival. If Linda could show God's love to masses of young people back in those days, then for us with all our 21st century tools like websites, social networks, and mobile communication there is absolutely no excuse not to do it.

Serge Velbovets
President of Global Christian Internet Network
InVictory.com

Linda's story is the story of God's unfailing grace and the power of a God given vision. Through it all, the vision has been tested and tried but has never died. Though Linda shares the historical account of her past, her eyes look steadfast to the future to see what God has yet to do in the world. The most powerful tool in the life of a believer is their testimony and Linda inspires testimony wherever she goes. May God bring the vision to pass in the city of Seattle.

Richard Vicknair

Pastor of Westside Church (Seattle)

Founder and International Director of

Worldcamp Kenya Relief International

Former Jesus People Army Leader

I first heard of Linda Meissner through Jim Palosaari, leader of the Milwaukee Jesus People. The accounts I heard first hand from him, confirm all that you will or have read in this challenging and inspiring book! Linda and I have both carried the same burden our entire life...."to make disciples for the Lord Jesus Christ!" As I have said thousands of times... "If you live for today... plant wheat...if you live for tomorrow...plant trees...BUT if you live for Eternity... TRAIN YOUNG MEN AND WOMEN TO PREACH THE GOSPEL" Linda Meissner lives for Eternity! We look forward to working with her again, to see "Joel's Army" come to pass! Welcome back LINDA!

William (Bill) Lowery
Evangelist and Founder of
Christ is the Answer Ministries

Though Linda Meissner has been through the fire, I believe 'these bones' shall rise again. I have shared with many, "When Linda returns to the vision given to her in Mexico City, she will see it fulfilled." God is the God of restoration. I know her heart, and the gifts of God in her life. I was there, walking alongside her for 10 years, including this great movement of Jesus People. The anointing she possessed was rare. Many have tried to tell this story, but they were not *The Voice*. I believe that after forty years of getting it right she will indeed rise again as a Deliverer among the youth of America.

Trena McDougal
Pastor, International Speaker
Former Jesus People Army Leader

Endorsements

The Voice, by Linda Meissner is a remarkable testimony about the Jesus People revival of the 60s and 70s, its ups and downs, and the dramatic events that shaped a new generation of Christians. It is also an urgent plea for the renewal of evangelism in our own day.

Dr Torbjorn Aronson
PhD in Government
ThD in Church History
Professor, Uppsala University, Sweden

I have known the author Linda Meisner for several years. She is a powerful woman, always full of life and the Holy Sprit. She has inspired me and I love to hear her testimonies from the Jesus Movement. I highly recommend her book *The Voice.* It is a voice for our generation that I believe will release a fresh move of God. I pray that you will be touched and revived as you read. This is not for a past season but for the season we are entering into now.

Christian Hedegaard
Evangelist, Denmark

I have the great privilege and honor to know Linda Meissner. Her life is a reflection of God's plan to send His grace to every person in every culture at any time. Her ministry has impacted different generations in a special way. Her book *The Voice* reveals the great work of God, that was executed by simple, open people and it presents an unforgettable story.

Vadim Privedenyuk
Pastor of Next Generation Christian Center

Jack Sparks, Duane Pederson, and Linda Meissner

Gallery

Linda Meissner with her only son, Dan Hegelund.

Dan Hegelund directing choir

The Voice

LINDA MEISSNER

Title: The Voice
Author: Linda Meissner
Editor: Dan Hegelund
Copyright © 2012 by Gloriana Publishing
Copyright © 2020 by FaithC Inc.
All rights reserved by FaithC Inc.
1st Edition
ISBN-13: 978-9198065404
ISBN-10: 9198065408

WWW.FAITHC.ORG
www.facebook.com/linda.meissner.7
linda_may7@hotmail.com, (425) 524-5531

Linda Meissner and Dan Hegelund now lead a ministry out of Spokane, WA. Visit www.faithc.org for more information.

The Voice

LINDA MEISSNER

The Voice

DEDICATION

*A good man leaves an inheritance
to his children's children...
Proverbs 13:22*

This book is dedicated to my only son, Dan Hegelund, to his wife, Marija, and to my beloved grandchildren, Emmanuel Luke, Evelyn Rose, and Victoria Daenerys.

The Voice

CONTENTS

FOREWORD BY DOUG PARRIS.............................. 21
1   OUT OF THE HEARTLAND...................... 27
2   GOD IS ALIVE.. 31
3   TO NEW YORK...................................... 35
4   THE CROSS AND THE SWITCHBLADE..... 39
5   BIG WEE.. 45
6   TRASHING LIFE...................................... 49
7   TEEN HARVESTERS TRIO....................... 53
8   THE FORBIDDEN CITY........................... 57
9   30 DOLLARS IN MY POCKET.................. 61
10   SEATTLE ON FIRE.................................. 65
11   JESUS REVOLUTION............................. 69
12   CARD-CARRYING COMMUNIST.............. 73
13   I SAW AN ARMY.................................... 77
14   CATACOMBS COFFEE HOUSE................. 79
15   BIRTH OF THE JESUS PEOPLE ARMY........ 83
16   SCHOOLS OPEN THEIR DOORS.............. 87
17   LIVING IN HELL..................................... 89
18   THE MONKEY STORY............................ 93
19   METH.. 97
20   SPIRITUAL REVOLUTION........................ 101
21   THE NEXT BEST THING.......................... 105
22   PUBLIC BAPTISMS................................. 109
23   SPOKANE... 113
24   BOISE.. 117
25   YAKIMA... 119
26   VANCOUVER... 123

27	EDMONTON	127
28	BACK TO SEATTLE	131
29	JESUS PEOPLE MOVEMENT	135
30	CHILDREN OF GOD	139
31	EUROPE	143
32	UTTERMOST PART OF THE EARTH	147
33	FORNICATION AND ADULTERY	149
34	A PUBLIC APOLOGY	153
35	THE OCCUPY MOVEMENT	155
36	RAISING MY SON	161
37	SCANDINAVIA	165
38	THE CALL	169
39	BOOT CAMP	173
40	THE VOICE	177
SINNER'S PRAYER		183
APPENDICES		185
	UPDATE 2020	185
	THE MISSION	186
	GOD'S LOVE LETTER TO YOU	189

ACKNOWLEDGMENTS

I am grateful for the voluntary contributions of Dan and Mary Hegelund, Doug Parris, Roberta Stephani, and Susan Palosaari Cowper, who assisted me at various editorial stages of the book. Thank you.

The Voice

FOREWORD
BY DOUG PARRIS

What you hold in your hand may be one of the most significant books of the last hundred years.

No single individual started the extraordinary cultural movement *Time Magazine* called the "Jesus Revolution" (once you discount Jesus, of course).

Spiritual stirrings sprang up in a thousand places across America in the late stages of the sixth decade of the twentieth century as God began to manifest himself unmistakably in supernatural ways; healing lives, healing sicknesses, and generally proving his own existence in enough ways to make a committed atheist gnash his teeth.

But the beginnings of that revival (albeit extraordinary) were not the "Jesus Revolution" any more than the many nondenominational mega-churches with contemporary music that grew up following its demise were, any longer, the "Jesus Revolution." It was something much more rare than revival.

For you the reader, who now hold *The Voice* in your hand, you deserve to be told that if the spiritual yearning in the hearts of young people in the late '60s and early '70s was the oxygen and the social and cultural unrest across the campuses of America during that same period was the fuel, then in fact a single individual—the author of the work you now hold—was the spark that ignited the explosion by the power of the Vision she said was given to her by the Creator.

I was privileged to observe first hand, for several years and from several vantage points, the amazing, seemingly inexplicable, and eventually even tragic work of Linda Meissner. I heard her radio ministry over the airwaves, heard her speeches as an anonymous face in the audience, and finally worked with and got to know her up close as a soldier and leader in her army, city by city and state by state. And by the measure of similarity to the accounts of the New Testament, her work was Apostolic and her Vision prophetic.

Linda spoke "...not with enticing words of man's wisdom" but simply and clearly, "in demonstration of the Spirit and of power." The inspiration that grew out of Linda's voice, (that we all then called "the Vision," long before David Wilkerson's book of the same title) was conceived, nurtured and brought to birth in different ways in different hearts. But everyone involved will tell you it was the contagious restoration, for that time, of first century Christianity.

This is by her own account, the personal story of the woman who lit the fires of the "Jesus Revolution," but it is much more than that.

The Movement that sprang up around Linda's Vision was at that time culturally revolutionary. It swept America in Christian Rock and folk music, chain-reaction evangelism, miracles and street ministry and it was eventually, though tentatively, christened the "Fourth Great Awakening" in many quarters by contemporary historians, thus equating it, in some measure, with the spiritual stirrings that culminated in the American Revolution (the First Great Awakening). But what occurred in the wake of its explosion in 1970s America (for all of us who were at its epicenter at the beginning) despite an impact on American Christianity and Politics measurable to this day, fell short of its own standards of achievement. The dry bones of dead fundamentalism did come together and stand upon their feet; many messengers "ran to and fro in the city" and "upon the rooftops;" and phalanxes of them did "tell the world of the soon-coming King"; but four decades after Linda's disappearance and separation from the Vision she had begun, there was still no "exceeding great Army" of spiritual revolutionaries as had been promised and predicted.

But it may be time to renew expectations of such an army of spiritual LOVE...

Because this historic figure is still alive and is returning from 40 years in the wilderness.

And she tells us the Vision will at last, be completed.

The Voice

And the LORD shall utter His voice
before His army...
Joel 2:11 (KJV)

The Voice

CHAPTER ONE

OUT OF THE HEARTLAND

I was raised on a farm in Iowa. I knew how to get milk out of a cow and how to ride horses. In fact, I had my own horse, named Lady. I loved to feed all the animals on the farm.

My dad taught me how to drive a tractor at the age of five, so I could help drive the pulley rope that carried bales of clover hay into the barn. When I was older, I helped prepare the fields for planting and in the fall bring in the harvest of corn and oats. My mom grew a garden full of healthy vegetables, and prepared nearly all our food all year around.

I was the oldest of four children. We loved to make homemade ice cream and candy. Our saddest Thanksgiving dinner was the one when halfway through the meal, Mother let us know it was our pet goose we were eating.

I was a swinging chick! There was not a teacher that I couldn't outsmart. I was good in sports. No one around could pitch a softball like me. I could swing that bat and empty the bases, bringing myself in as a home run. Then there was music. I won a state contest, singing *Morning has Broken.*

I had everything going my way. I didn't need nothing or nobody. As far as I knew, God could do nothing for teenagers.

I had a little grandmother who always used to tell me, " Honey, I want you to read the Bible." So, out of respect, I opened up the dull old book, and I read the Bible. To my surprise, it was fascinating!

I read about a Jesus that opened up blind eyes. I read about a Jesus who made lame people walk. I read about a Jesus who fed 5,000 people with just a few loaves and fishes.

And then I went to church, and not a thing happened.

I went to a little Methodist church. Every Sunday you could see me there with my family. Older youth would talk about the shows they'd seen or dances they'd been to.

We sat in a pew and listened to some man tell us about a God that was 40,000 miles away, that was able to do something 2000 years ago. It did not relate to me. Somehow, I made it through the boring service.

I used to take long walks under the stars, down the old gravel road that led to the English River, just to think about all this. I just couldn't understand why such a big God in the Bible was such a dead God in the church.

Then one day, my mother fell sick and was taken away. The report was that she might not live.

The Voice

CHAPTER TWO

GOD IS ALIVE

My dad spent a lot of money on doctors, trying to bring my mother back to health. It seemed to me no one could help her.

One day I stood out on the porch of our old farm house and looked across the corn fields. I looked at a beautiful sunset, and I said to myself, "Friends and popularity can't help me. Money can't help. It is going to take something powerful to get me back my mother."

I marched into my bedroom.

"Hey, look God," I said, "if you're up there, I'd like to know if you couldn't come here and do something for me. God, I don't really know how to talk to you."

Then I opened up my Bible. There was Matthew 7:7. It told me "Ask, and it will be given to you."

My, that was easy! I had thought religion was hard. I looked up and said, "OK God, touch my mom and make her alright."

But I realized anyone can come to God when they have a problem. I was not being quite fair. What God really wanted was me. I stood there and I said, "Alright God, forgive me, I receive you, and you can have me."

Later on, when I was working with the gangs in New York, I talked to a girl on the street corner one day. She prayed right there on the street and asked God to come into her life. She said, "Linda, do you know how I feel just now? Well, it feels like a bubble bath on the inside!" That's the way I felt that day I let God have me.

Then I knew He wasn't "dead." It wasn't a philosophy. It wasn't a religion. I could feel Him. You know what? I've been able to feel Him every day since!

God touched my mother and made her well.

She was a good Christian woman, and we had many good times together around the piano singing good ol' hymns she knew. If God could do that for me, He could do that for anybody. So, I decided to go to Bible school and study the Bible. My Dad sold my own cow, Sugar, to get the money for me to go.

The Voice

CHAPTER THREE

TO NEW YORK

I went to Central Bible College in Springfield, Missouri. It was there I first heard about a "baptism of power" like the apostles received in Acts 2:4. One evening as I was seeking God down at the altar, He gave me that baptism, with the evidence of speaking in another tongue.

Not long after that, I was once again down at the altar in the school chapel. I had an experience. I sure hadn't been using LSD or marijuana. No, this experience was a vision from God. I saw before me a great big canyon with flaming fire, smoke, and jagged rock. Above, on a cliff, there were hundreds of young people. Then a man came by with a big long chain, and he bound the young peoples' ankles together and wrapped the chain around them so they could not go free. Another man came by, picked them up and threw them with the weight of their body over the cliff into the giant gorge.

I heard them scream.

It was the most horrible scream I had ever heard. When the vision went away, I was just kneeling there and words came to me that have come to many others. "I have only one life, it can go quickly past. Only what I do for God will last." I made up my mind that night that I was going to go everywhere and tell teenagers that "Jesus Christ is the real 'In crowd,' He is 'what's happening;' if you don't want to scream like that some day, you'd better give your life to God!"

One day we had had a united school assembly to hear a special speaker. On the stage was a skinny little man. He introduced himself as David Wilkerson. None of us had heard him speak before or knew who he was. He began to tell an amazing story of how God took him from being a pastor in a little country church to the New York City streets, where he spoke to organized gangs and drug addicts. He told us how God had touched gang leaders such as Nicky Cruz, whose entire gangs of Mau Maus turned to Jesus.

He had on his heart to get a big house to start a center where youth could come for help, and even live there to be strengthened in their God walk. He said he needed workers alongside him to get this job done.

I felt the Holy Spirit in me as he spoke. Afterwards, the college president said that anyone who wished to speak to Dave could meet him in the library. So I did and became one of the first workers to help David Wilkerson in New York Teen Challenge. I was a prominent figure in his best-selling book *The Cross and the Switchblade.*

The Voice

CHAPTER FOUR

THE CROSS AND THE SWITCHBLADE

In New York I met Nicky Cruz, former vice president of the Mau Mau gang, as well as other ex-gang members and former junkies. We formed a team to reach needy New York youth for Jesus! My job was to lead the work with the organized girl gangs, which were called the Dolls and Debs.

I knew my life would be in danger.

Each morning all workers met in the chapel. Dave would share from the Word, and then we all prayed for an hour or two. At twelve noon we ate together, then had another prayer meeting. Only after that, did we go out to speak to people in the streets from two until six. Then we took a short break at whatever location we were in, to eat a packed sandwich, before continuing work. When we came back to the Teen Challenge Center at around 7:30 we held an open service for youth in the chapel, often until midnight.

I felt a deep fear inside as I walked the dirty streets of Brooklyn with their unkempt apartment buildings, un-emptied garbage cans, and broken windows. I saw many gang kids. They wore leather jackets, black leather boots, and shades. Some of them came up out of the subway, carrying umbrellas in their hands. The ends of those umbrellas had been sharpened like knives.

I knew the gangsters could kill me.

They wore tattoos with devils, demons, and various monsters. Some wore black bandanas while others wore Stetson cowboy hats. I knew they were "bopping" and "jitter bugging," their slang for street fighting. They were stabbing people in the lungs with their switchblades. Killings were a regular occurrence. And my partner and I (we always went in twos) were talking to them about God right there on their "turf," by the bars, or wherever they were.

I'll never forget I was talking to four dolls and debs one day. One of them took a long drag off her cigarette, blew smoke in my face and said, "That's what I think of you."

I said, "Thanks a lot, but you know something? I love you. God loves you. He wants to change your life. He wants to give you a new beginning."

Yes, at first they all were mean, but they soon started melting and being nice and saying, "You're right, Linda, we have a lot of hang-ups, and we don't know how to get rid of them. Linda, will you pray for us?" So, we prayed right there on the street corner. You could feel God right there, and He began coming into those gang girls.

As evening fell, two big gang leaders came by. They looked me over and said, "Hey, baby, you're looking fine. How about spending the night with us?"

I said, "No thank-you."

They said, "What's wrong, you afraid?"

I said, "No, I don't believe in that." They marched away, and they were mad, but I never thought anything serious was happening.

A few minutes later I heard a loud cry! I knew that was the sound of a gang "rumble." I turned around quickly to see if they were going to stab someone and split the scene before the cops came. As I turned around, I saw a big shining knife, sharp as a razor, heading right for me. Somehow God helped me instantly turn again —just enough so that the knife ripped through my clothes, but missed cutting my body. The two gang leaders had returned but this time with their gang.

Behind us was a big red building, but otherwise, we were surrounded by gang members. I knew what happened to "little girls" who got caught out on New York streets alone. We were caught completely off guard.

Then I said to the leader of the gang, "God bless you." When I said that, he lifted his hand saying, "Something is different about these girls, we'd better let them go." They took their hands off me, and I walked calmly across the street. They did not bother me again. I walked quickly back to the Teen Challenge Center. Was I ever glad to be safely home! I had just witnessed being protected by the power of God.

Another time we had been working 5th Avenue. There were about five organized gangs within the area of a few blocks. I remember every Monday night we were meeting at a particular corner under a certain tree. There we talked to dopers, gangsters, and prostitutes about Jesus.

I remember feeling that on this particular night, we should *not* meet as usual under the tree. Instead, I felt we should go out witnessing two by two, and that we did. Come to find out, there had been a homemade bomb planted under that tree. They had planned to blow us to bits, but we weren't there!

When I went to "Negro" Harlem, I was told, "If you come in here, we'll kill you." One day I heard someone say, "Can I ask you a question?" and turned to see a tall black militant. First, he cursed me because I was a Christian. Then he cursed me because my skin was the wrong color. I was completely surrounded by black militants. He asked, "Do you know what we're going to do with you now?" I had heard that the week before they had cut out a human heart and displayed it on a platter for everyone to see. They said that they would do that to me, if I came into their territory. I waited calmly quite a while, before I said, "God bless you." The God that parted the Red Sea for the Children of Israel, parted the black sea for me. I walked right through and they never touched me.

The Voice

CHAPTER FIVE

BIG WEE

Teen Challenge included gang kids from many different areas of the city. There were the Dragons, the Hell Burners, the Mau Maus, the Chaplins, the Assassin Lords, etc. We held special meetings just for them in our big house at 316 Clinton Avenue, Brooklyn, New York. In reality, the different gangs hated each other.

One night our chapel was full. The different gang members were glaring back and forth at each other. We had a pretty little girl come sing us a song. They laughed and whistled at her. That night, it seemed everything we did went wrong. Finally, one of our guys,

I will call him Preacher Boy, got up and walked back and forth across the front of the room. He told the gang members, "You know something, I'm going to tell you guys plain like it is. Every one of you guys here are such big dads are you? The truth is you are nothing but cowards and chicken. Big Wee, you are the biggest chicken of them all."

You may get by calling people "chicken" in some places, but you don't get by calling New York gang members "chicken." Those guys reached for their knives as they stood up. They were ready to jump Preacher Boy. Then Big Wee, the president of the Hell Burners, stood up and said, "That's right, I'm a chicken, sit down!" And they all sat down. Then the young man in the front began to walk back and forth again. He looked them all square in the face and said, "You know something? You guys in here are so tough are you? You're cowards. You let a little three-inch stick be your boss. You don't even have the guts to pronounce the word 'no.' You boast about your indulgence in shameful sex. You boast about your drunken hangovers. You boast about all the times you've gotten stoned, and all the girls you've gotten in trouble, and all the places you've broken into. Think of all the people you've hurt. You don't have the knowledge to know the biggest person you're hurting is yourself! And Big Wee, you are the biggest chicken of them all."

The boys were glaring mad! They reached for their knives again and stood up, ready to fight. I was afraid it was the end. Big Wee stood up once again and said, "Sit down." They all sat down.

Then Preacher Boy continued, "You guys are so weak that in fact you can't even carry a Bible. More than that, it is one thing to get started on the wrong foot in life, but you do not have what it takes to look up at the One who made you, and say, 'Hey, God, I'm sorry, please forgive me, and give me a new beginning.' Or, to tell people you have hurt, 'I'm sorry'."

He continued, "Big Wee, you are the president of the Hell Burners, and you are the biggest chicken of them all." Then everyone simply stood and marched out!

A few minutes later there came a knock on the door. Big Wee was standing there with his hands folded. I asked him what he wanted. He was insulted! "What do you mean, what do I want? I came to get your God. That's what you want me to do, ain't it?" He marched into the chapel, pulled out a chair, and got down on his knees. I heard a few sniffles and saw tears running down his face. He prayed out, "Oh, God forgive me for all the wrong things I've done. I believe Jesus died for my sins. I receive him. Give me a second chance."

God completely changed his life. His vice-president got saved and almost half his gang found God that night. They changed their switchblades for the cross of Jesus Christ!

CHAPTER SIX

TRASHING LIFE

Another time, my witnessing partner and I were walking down a particularly dirty street in Brooklyn. We heard a cry that made us look at each other. Together we walked over to an old garbage can along the side of a building. Yes, the cry was coming from there!

Lifting the lid, we saw a little baby, naked and squalling! Someone had evidently decided they didn't want it and simply threw it away. I called David, who called the New York police; officers came and took the infant from my arms. Somewhere today, I believe there's a person who will never know her almost tragic end.

We had been on our way to talk to a girl we'd met the day before. When we finally arrived, we walked up the stairs of the old apartment building and knocked on the door. No one answered. I knocked harder. As I did, I thought I could smell gas. Then I banged on the door 'til it flew open. There on the floor our girl had passed out. She'd turned on the gas burner, trying to trash her own life. I called Dave and told him the latest situation we'd encountered. These were the days when you had to find a phone booth on a corner! Dave sent an ambulance while we stayed with the girl, helping her get fresh air, glad that we had come in time to interrupt another tragedy!

God saved one from infanticide... one from suicide. But you can also throw your life away little by little.

I remember another girl, Kathy. As I began to share with her, she started to scream like she was going out of her mind. I said, "I don't mean to harm you."

She yelled, "Get away from me, Linda. Don't talk to me." When I asked her what was wrong, she told me her story.

"Now I am going to tell you something you won't believe." She continued, "Do you know such and such church? Well, I used to sing in the choir. I used to be full of God. I could feel God's presence in me from the top of my head to the soul of my feet. I loved to spend all day Sunday in the church. But, Linda, I got tired of praying. I got tired of going to church. I got tired of being a 'goody goody.' They told me I ought to try the discotheques. They insisted I get drunk on beer or wine. They kept at me to try 'fun' things. I got to listening to them, and they began to eat my mind. Linda, I tried the first thing, and I didn't confess it. I tried the second thing, it caught up on me. I tried the third thing, and I just got in deeper and deeper. It was like I was standing on quick sand and sinking down. Linda, do you see that girl in the corner over there in the tight pants wearing a shirt and boots?"

The girl was pacing back and forth like an animal in a cage.

"Linda, you won't believe it, but I have been sleeping with that girl for eight months. I am a homosexual. I will never feel God again. How can God ever forgive me? Linda, do me a favor. Just one favor. Tell the young people to the north, south, east and west, that if they don't keep their lives covered with the blood of Jesus, the devil will do everything he can to destroy them. The devil is no respecter of persons. He doesn't care what color you are, or if you are a church goer, or who you are, he wants to destroy you!"

She ran off before I got the chance to pray with her.

Whoever you are, reading this story, you need to have your life covered with Jesus' blood and grace. God is not dead. What He did for me, and for Big Wee, He wants to do for you. Now, just bow your head with me, and let's talk to the man upstairs about it. You only have to do two things. Confess your sins, and invite Jesus into your life.

Jesus, look at that guy or that girl right now, and forgive them. They are really sorry. Take their sins away. They are opening their heart to you, come into their life and show them how much you love them. Thank you, God, for doing this. In Jesus' name.

CHAPTER SEVEN

TEEN HARVESTERS TRIO

While visiting my grandmother in Bakersfield, California, she asked me to share with the women in her church the amazing stories from New York. Then they asked if I would speak again on Sunday night at a big youth meeting. I was a bit frightened, but agreed. That night God just talked through me and at the end, the young people were down at the altar crying out to God. Then one by one, pastors came up to ask me to speak in their churches. From then on, I had a full speaking schedule. I traveled throughout the United States, speaking in churches and camps, conventions and Full Gospel Business meetings.

One night after preaching in El Paso, Texas, I gave an altar call. A few came to pray and I had a tremendously heavy burden. I spoke out, "Someone is here tonight, who needs to get right with God. You have run away from him, but he is calling you back right now." A tall Spanish girl stood up and ran to the altar. She cried and cried. That night Rebecca Lozano got right with God.

During a meeting in Bakersfield, California, I met another young girl named Trena Layman. At that time she was engaged to be married and had already bought her wedding dress. One evening when she was cooking supper she heard a voice call out her name, "Trena, Trena." She looked around, supposing it was her dad. However, he wasn't there. She continued cooking, but again heard her name being called. This time she walked through the house to see if her dad was there. He was not. She went back to the kitchen where she heard a voice call out her name loud and clear, "Trena, Trena." Then she knew it was the voice of the Lord calling her in a different direction. She fell to her knees and said, "Yes, Lord, here I am, send me." She broke the engagement and answered the call of God on her life.

Some time later I invited both Trena and Rebecca to join me to form an evangelistic team. We called ourselves the "Teen Harvesters Trio." We spent one summer with Teen Challenge New York. Then we began to travel all over the United States, singing and speaking. Rebecca played the piano. I preached, and both girls gave powerful testimonies. Everywhere we went God used us to touch the hearts of the youth. Occasionally we teamed up with David Wilkerson.

The Voice

CHAPTER EIGHT

THE FORBIDDEN CITY

When we received an invitation from the Full Gospel Business Men to travel to Asia, my heart almost skipped a beat. I had always dreamt about seeing the world, so without hesitation Trena and I said yes!

While in Hong Kong, Trena and I went to Kowloon Walled City, where the "untouchables" and the social outcasts lived. It was called the Forbidden City. We walked through its narrow streets where hardly any light from the sun shone. It was poverty like we had never seen. The worst was the sight of the opium dens with men of all ages sitting along the side of the streets smoking their opium pipes. A local missionary took us to the city prison, where all the prisoners were convicted murderers, sentenced to life imprisonment. We were allowed to stand right in the midst of them. They may have been murderers, but when I spoke and they heard the gospel these men began to weep like babies, and before long they prayed the sinner's prayer. They spontaneously lifted their hands towards heaven and began to thank Jesus who had just forgiven all their sins.

In Taiwan we saw Buddhist temples, where people of every age were praying out loud, and offered food and incense to their gods. I was asked to dedicate a new church for the aboriginal people of Taiwan. Our truck followed the narrow, bumpy road winding around the mountain. We had to get out of the truck and walk the last part of the way. We were welcomed by the most unusual of sights. Aborigines with tattooed charcoal face markings and missing teeth, and big nose rings and earrings. I was nearly afraid, as they ushered us into their church building. But oh, how their prayers and praises rang loud and clear! I felt the Holy Spirit really strong, and understood that they were really my brothers and sisters.

In South Korea I had the honor to visit several churches. Many of them had no heat or seats. Still the people would come several hours before the service began, just to pray. They brought little mats and sat on the ground or floor. Tears poured from their eyes as they prayed. One church had a congregation of 7,000 with 100 elders to help the pastor in different sections of Seoul. I attended a camp meeting where over 2,000 met in the mountains for ten days to fast and pray. Prayers could be heard all night long. Even though they worked long, hard days, scores of them were up in the morning to pray anywhere from two to five hours asking God to send revival. I thought that maybe the Korean believers needed to send missionaries to America!

The Voice

CHAPTER NINE

30 DOLLARS IN MY POCKET

I was so touched by seeing thousands in The Philippines' Manila Square. They were starving to hear the good news of the Gospel. After I spoke in the Square, hundreds responded to the Gospel. A little later I returned to that nation—alone.

Here is how Rev. Paul Pipkin described it:

"A vigorous 60-day crusading in the Philippines left Linda tired, but happy. She preached two and three times a day nearly every day.

"A Baptist minister was filled with the Holy Spirit in Iligan City. American servicemen were saved in Olongapo. Filipino youth gang members were converted in Caloocan. Students were converted in school rallies in many places. How did it happen?

"Linda admitted she was just a farm girl, but with a twinkle in her eye she said, "That's why we have the Holy Spirit... what we can't do ourselves, we just yield to the Lord Jesus, and the Spirit through us does the work."

"Linda Meissner came to the Philippines unannounced. In fact, no one in the Department of Evangelism expected her. Linda's only reason for coming, she explained, was "Jesus told me to come." Yet, she confessed she only had 30 dollars to her name and no return fare to the USA. How could this person be so daring in times like these? It all seemed too simple and innocent for these complex days, yet here she was."

"I was scheduled to speak at a Sunday afternoon CA Rally, but I decided to step aside and test the spirit of our surprise evangelist. It was immediately evident her spirit was burning with zeal for Christ and for souls, but I wondered if this little lady was rugged enough to rough it... could she eat the local food and take the tropical climate? To some extent my fears melted away as I listened to her testimony and watched the Filipino youth respond. After the challenge, I suggested to the pastors present in the rally to invite our guest evangelist for crusades in their churches. However, I told them she had no money, therefore all the responsibility for her personal room and expenses for the crusade promotion would have to be theirs to assume."

"The Filipinos welcomed her into their homes, churches, and schools. She ate their food and slept where they put her. Linda's willingness to accept and be thankful for whatever came her way was only outmatched by Filipino hospitality and sacrifice to serve her."

"All too soon, the time has flown. Many more pastors wanted her to come. However, Linda now feels it is time for her to return to the U.S.A. "If God wills, and if Jesus says so" she will return to the Philippines. Linda leaves now with the satisfaction she did what the Lord told her to do and proved victoriously, God is able to make a way through every obstacle."

"She blessed the congregations in Caloocan, Quezon City, Malinta, Bethel Bible Institute, Chi Alpha, Olongapo, Iligan City, Tondo and others. She has been a faith tonic and an inspiration to all who heard her testimony."

"Concerning her Philippine experiences, Linda said, 'I loved every minute. They treated me like a queen sent from heaven. Their hospitality was beyond words. I've never been so happy in my life.'"

"'Oh yes," she added, 'I have the same 30 dollars. I did not spend them.'" Filipino love offerings came in for her local expenses, and Linda's return fare was sent in from three friends in the USA exactly on the deadline date to buy her ticket within her visa time limit." (*Pentecostal Voice*, November 1967)

CHAPTER TEN

SEATTLE ON FIRE

Our trio continued to travel. We preached and sang throughout much of California. Then a letter arrived from Roy Johnson, pastor of Seattle, Washington's Philadelphia church. He asked if we girls would come to Seattle for a three-day revival meeting. We decided to go. The Holy Spirit moved in a very powerful way. Soon many other churches in Seattle and the surrounding area asked us to hold revival services, the result being that Seattle's Church youth caught on fire for God!

I came up with the idea of starting a Teen Challenge Center in Seattle. This idea was supported by a Full Gospel Fellowship Executive Board of eight Pastors, and a

Teen Challenge Board of six pastors from the Seattle area. The Teen Harvester Trio (Trena McDougal, Becky Lozano and myself) were part of the full time staff, and many students from Northwest College and from different churches helped with this important project.

One day while in deep prayer, I had a very vivid vision. Jesus was stretching his hands out over the city of Seattle. I heard the words of a song deep in my spirit, "There He stands with healing in His wings. Hope for all who know the way of care." I understood this vision to mean that I was to look at the entire city and its people, not just to the drug addicts.

It is good to build a hospital at the bottom of a cliff, so that when the children fall off there is a hospital to fix them. However, it is better to build a fence around the mountain cliff, so that the children don't fall down to the bottom far below in the first place.

Because of this vision I stopped working with Teen Challenge. The Teen Challenge Center continued and does so even to this day. I began instead to look for a place from which I could reach out to *all* Seattle's youth, not just drug addicts. I found a good location at 1618 North 45th. I called it *The Ark*. It served as a counseling and training center and headquarters for our nightly witnessing teams.

I sent out applications to interested youth using the mailing list from my speaking engagements. Applications came in from Spirit-filled youth of various denominations in the greater Seattle area. Together they formed a tremendous witnessing force of approximately 60 young people. Every afternoon and evening, organized teams invaded the parks, beaches, projects, University District, and the Seattle Center. The burden these youth had, moved them to action. They dedicated their lives that summer to full time outreach to save the youth of Seattle.

Cheryl Estep shares, "I first heard of Linda as a teenager, when I read 'The Cross and the Switchblade.' The story deeply touched my life. But, I never imagined then, that I personally would know Linda. During my time in Bible College, the Teen Harvester Trio, Linda, Trena, and Becky, came and spoke in various churches in my home town. There I met and heard Linda preach. It really moved me. The Trio took us out street witnessing. After that I joined a team that went out witnessing every week-end. I remember seeing teens, really young teens, 13 and 14, who were totally disillusioned with life. They had a haunted look in their eyes, like they had tried everything and there was nothing left to live for. This was really shocking to me, to see this look in people so young. I remember feeling such a burden to reach them. I was trying to talk to them, but I couldn't seem to relate to them.

"Then one night at church, I went forward for prayer, and I just told the Lord, I needed help in breaking through to reach these kids. I could really feel their need, and I knew they needed the LORD. I felt like I was failing, I wasn't able to reach them, and I just couldn't go on not being able to reach them. Then that night as I was praying, I had a vision of Jesus. He was standing in front of me with His arms out, and love was just pouring out of Him. He gave me the scripture, "Behold the Lamb of God, which taketh away the sins of the world." (John 1:29) He showed me He was not here to condemn me or to condemn them. He was the Lamb of God who came to take away our sins. All we needed to do was to come to Him and repent. He was there to love us and restore us and to forgive us. Then that love radiating out of Jesus began pouring into me. I just drank it in, and drank it in. Then the vision left. He spoke that His Love was the most powerful force in the world. That was what I needed to reach those kids."

CHAPTER ELEVEN

JESUS REVOLUTION

Every year one of Seattle's leading rock stations sponsored a teenage fair at the Seattle Center. Everything from body painting to psychedelic posters were available. Several acid rock groups attracted 80,000 youth to the Seattle Coliseum. In the midst of the devil's playground, God gave us an exhibition area, for "Youth Speaks Spiritual Revolution."

We used a religious survey to identify those interested in a personal relationship with Jesus. Our invasion teams from *The Ark* were able to personally contact over 3,000 teenagers. Dozens of youth found Christ daily and several were filled with the Holy Spirit. It was the most popular place at the fair, because the kids said it was the only booth that presented reality. The crowning event was when God performed a miracle before the eyes of many amazed young people as they watched a young man's leg grow out.

In addition to *The Ark*, I started a weekly radio program called "Youth Speaks." I had young people speak and share what God had done for them. The show was popular among the Jesus People. Everyone knew where to tune in, and when! The impact of the radio station cannot be overstated. It was one of the true instruments of the revival that was already under way.

Doug Parris explains:

"When Linda Meissner took the stage in late '60s America, it was as if someone had darkened the house and turned on the spotlight.

The room went silent.

I remember where I was the first time I heard her voice. It was close to the intersection of North 185th Street and Wallingford Avenue in Seattle, 40 blocks north of the city limits. I don't know what I was doing or the destination to which I was driving, but the radio was on and a voice I'd never heard came through the speaker.

Linda was not shriller nor louder than what had preceded (and followed) her nor did she dazzle me with rhetorical gymnastics. But something was extraordinarily dynamic. She was challenging Marxism, and it was like being awakened by a baptism of ice water. No one had ever said these things before.

And now here, on my car radio, in a voice that could have been Janis Joplin, was a young woman asserting that there were *no answers* in Karl Marx—that the only comprehensive answer for the troubles of the World was the ability to transform human nature that dwelt bodily in Jesus Christ. She asserted the power and presence of actual miracles and the joy of living, not in chemical-induced euphoria, but by the flow of the Holy Spirit, and a plan underway to change the world through spiritual revolution. He could transform all of society."

Doug continues, "I had been born on the campus of a major Christian College to two of its faculty members. My father had his PhD in Biblical Theology and hosted a "Bible Answers" radio program. I "accepted the Lord" at the age of four, went to kindergarten with the children of Billy Graham staffers, went to church three times a week and had grown up backstage – a pastor's kid in the evangelical, Biblical, protestant church – and I had never heard anyone talk like Linda Meissner. The whole of the protestant church was dead by comparison. She was a true revolutionary.

71

Within the next three years (through events in which I participated) and totally without financing, her Vision swept the United States and became one of *Look Magazine's* Top Ten News Stories of 1971.

For the Lord had uttered his voice before his army."

CHAPTER TWELVE

CARD–CARRYING COMMUNIST

All up and down the west coast there were underground newspapers, spreading the ideas of Karl Marx. It soon became clear that we also needed an underground newspaper to be able to combat the communist literature, and to tell about the spiritual revolution that was happening. We initially called it *Agape*, because it is the Greek word for 'divine love.' God is love in action. Our paper was full of stories from young people who had had their lives changed through the agape, or divine love, of God. Later, we changed the name to *The Truth* and eventually had a circulation of 100,000.

The *Agape* was distributed over the entire city of Seattle, as well as surrounding cities. Our Jesus People could be seen standing on many street corners with the paper in hand. We also distributed the paper in schools. We used our newspaper to help reach young people with the Love of God and to combat the influence of "hippie" newspapers like Seattle's "Helix," Bellingham's "Northwest Passage," and the "Spokane Natural", that wrote about the hippie drug, music, and sex culture from a Marxist point of view.

Bud Moegling explains, "I was a card carrying communist. I sought love through drugs. I played guitar in a music spot called the Pamir House in Seattle. The first time I got stoned I fainted, or flashed, hence the nickname, Flash. I had a psychedelic dance business and great plans, but one night I had a soul-searching vision in my room. This resulted in my business stopping. I had made a decision for Christ in 1966, but soon got sucked back into the hippie scene. I tried to run and deny my guilt and loneliness. I ran for three years on drugs, amphetamines, and an occasional smack (heroin) hit. My hatred for the world grew. I climbed the underground ladder as a disk jockey at KOL-FM. But, I kept running into Christians! Young girls with so much light in their eyes I couldn't face them."

"Then on a visit to California, I discovered God was moving really fast. Many of my friends from my high school days were serving the LORD and living together in brother and sister communities. When I returned to Seattle in the spring, I was a fanatical soul-winner."

Bud and I worked together on many occasions in Seattle. He was one of the frontline fighters God used to bring in revival to the state of Washington. Both his picture and testimony were in the first edition of the *Agape*.

We also used t-shirts to spread our message. Yes, the Jesus People had many of our slogans written on shirts, jackets, buttons, and bumper stickers. *Not Religion, Relationship with Jesus Christ!*, *PTL Praise The LORD!*, and the famous picture of a lifted finger pointing up to God with the inscription: *ONE WAY*! The entire Jesus movement up and down the west coast of America used this sign. Thousands and thousands of Jesus People.

We also had our song of unity:

> "We are one in the Spirit. We are one in the LORD.
> We are one in the Spirit. We are one in the LORD.
> And we pray that our unity may this day be restored.
> And, they'll know we are Christians by our love by our love. Yes, they'll know we are Christians by our love."

CHAPTER THIRTEEN

I SAW AN ARMY

In 1969 I was in Mexico City to speak. As usual, I began the day in prayer. It was not uncommon for me to pray for several hours. During this particular day, I was prostrate on the floor in the Spirit. The power and presence of the LORD was heavily upon me. I had been in His presence for hours, when I was given a vision: **A vision of an army of young people being raised up to take the gospel of Jesus Christ to their generation.** I saw a coffee house and exactly how it was to be made, and how it was to function. The instructions came to me almost as God instructed Noah how and why to build an ark.

The message was clear. Coffee houses and an army of young people going everywhere with the good news of Jesus!

When I returned to Seattle with my new instructions, it was clear to me that I could not accomplish this vision in my own wisdom or strength. I had always depended on the LORD, but now I really needed Him to do it!

I began to look for a coffee house location. I found it in downtown Seattle at First and Madison. For $130 dollars a month we could have this large building. We signed the contract by faith, and three days later we opened our new coffee house, *The Eleventh Hour*.

We were open every Friday and Saturday night from 9 pm to 1 am. Besides doughnuts and coffee we also offered live music, with several Christian bands, including our own Solid Rock Band led by Rex Parker. I spoke every night, and many found Jesus in this place!

We opened just before Seattle's famous Seafair festival. A U.S. Navy Fleet arrived at Pier 91 and the hustlers and prostitutes were out in full force to welcome the sailors. But so were we! The sailors were invited to *The Eleventh Hour*. The sailors were really ambushed by angels of death and life that day. Happily, many chose life.

CHAPTER FOURTEEN

CATACOMBS COFFEE HOUSE

One day a nice looking lady came to me and said,   "
Linda, this youth work and what is actually happening
here is too fantastic to be in this location. You need a
bigger place that is more centrally located." I did not know
who she was. I also knew talk is cheap. Some days later
she came to see me, "Linda, I think I have found the
perfect place for you. Do you have the time to come and
look at it?"

We drove straight to the Seattle Center. Towering over us
was the Space Needle. She parked the car. "It's right here,"
she said excitedly. She pointed to a large empty
warehouse on 5th and John. She had already talked to the

owner, and told him about the lives of young people being changed in a powerful and positive way by God. He was very favorable and had said yes to the idea of us making a Christian Coffee House there. So it was. The keys to the location were put in my hand!

We went inside. It had been an old warehouse, alright. It was full of junk and dirt. There was nothing in it we could use. However, we became very excited as we walked around in it. We could hardly wait to tell the young people working in *The Eleventh Hour* all about it!

Dirt and Nothingness were No Problem! We set a day for cleaning and Seattle's youth arrived with brooms, mops and buckets, cleaning rags, window cleaner, soap, etc. Everyone found a job to do, including boys who carried out unwanted items, and a father who helped organize them. We worked for many hours, but we were singing, and laughing, and talking, and having so Much FUN!

Someone said, "We need to paint this place. I know a local paint shop. I'll just walk in and tell the owner who we are, and what we are making, and ask if he would like to give us some paint to do the job." God gave us favor. The owner of the paint store was very impressed with what we were doing and gave us enough paint for the entire coffee house.

The bakery that had given us free donuts when we were at *The Eleventh Hour*, provided donuts for our new place across from the Seattle Center.

We called it *The Catacombs Coffee House!*

The days that followed were exciting indeed. "This place should have a stage," declared one young boy. Before I knew what was happening, he arrived with his father and some friends carrying in lumber to build a stage. They had all the tools needed and built a great stage opposite the entrance. Another boy piped up, "It needs to be covered with carpet." He talked to a carpet shop owner, and amazingly, we were given enough carpet to cover our stage and to lay wall-to-wall carpet in our prayer room.

The whole thing was a Great Sight! Painters were painting, there was building, laying of carpet, constant cleaning and singing. Then someone said, "Now all we need is a beautiful painting on the wall behind the stage." And, of course, there was one who could do that and was thrilled to use his talent for God! I remember how Trena Mc Dougal crunched up hundreds of brown paper grocery bags and glued them to the back of the stage wall to emulate rocks–providing a cave-like appearance carrying out *The Catacombs* theme.

One of the last challenges was tables. Then came the bright idea... We could use the spools that wire is wrapped around. So it was... Yes, we could have as many spools as we wanted, "Yes, you may borrow my parents' truck to take them to the coffee house," "Yes, you may have different colors of paint to paint them with," "Yes, you can have all the chairs you need." It was clear to me that God was "DOING IT!" Next we built a serving counter and made a sign for the *The Catacombs* and were ready to begin the real purpose of the coffee house!

CHAPTER FIFTEEN

BIRTH OF THE JESUS PEOPLE ARMY

I knew the music group, The Glorious Liberty, from Saint Luke's church in Seattle. They would be the perfect ones to sing on our new stage opening night. We also planned a sing-a-long where I would lead our own favorite songs with my tambourine and everyone at the club could join in the songs.

It was so cozy with little lights on each table. Everybody loved drinking coffee or tea while there was music coming from the stage. The little hole in the middle of the spool tables made a great donation box, and I needed only to say, "You can put a donation in the opening in the center of your table, if you like to."

I never needed to speak again about money.

After the singing, I always spoke. I spoke The Good News, "Jesus really loves You. Jesus died on the cross to pay the price for your sins and mistakes. He is not dead. He rose from the grave and is alive. He knows all about you and has a wonderful plan for your life. If you receive Him, He will give you a new beginning. He has the power to change your life no matter what your present situation is. Even if you are on drugs or an alcoholic, He will make you free from your old lifestyle, and will give you forgiveness, peace, joy, hope, and eternal life. All things become new!"

When I had finished speaking, I asked everyone to bow their heads. "I am going to pray now," I would say. "But, before I do, I want to ask if there is anyone here, who would like to receive Jesus? If you want to say yes to Jesus tonight, just raise your hand."

"Yes, I see one hand. Is there anyone else? Yes, I see two more hands go up. Is there anyone else here who would like to make the important decision tonight to receive Jesus? Yes, I see the four people who raised their hands at that table over there."

When it was clear there were no more hands to be raised, I would say, "Let us all pray this prayer together. Repeat after me: 'Jesus, here I am. Forgive my sins. Come into my life, I receive you now. Give me a new start. I believe in You and your words, and want to serve you all the days of my life. Amen."

I then asked each person who had raised their hand to follow me into the prayer room. Then as I walked toward the prayer room, the people who had raised their hand would follow after me. There were benches all the way around this room with its wall-to-wall carpet. There would be people there to help them pray to God, and to talk with them about Jesus. In this room is where the real spiritual revolution was born.

All in this room would really pray! Tears were a frequent occurrence. Here youth who had been using drugs were set free. The chains of alcohol were broken. The lonely found a close friend in Jesus (and us). Miracles happened here. One by one youth came to know God! No matter the background, whether from a church or "good family," university, or from the street. The youth of Seattle were turning on to Jesus!

The one became twelve. The twelve became twenty-four. The twenty-four became forty-eight. The forty-eight became a hundred, which soon became hundreds, and then thousands. Between 1000 and 2000 youth attended *The Catacombs Coffee House* each weekend.

Each weekend at *The Catacombs* people gave personal testimonies about what God had done for them. Jesus bands and single artists shared their music and dynamic speakers came forward to share the gospel. I never could have done without Trena McDougal. She was my right hand woman, and a leader in the Jesus People Army. Robert Sirico spoke regularly at the Catacombs while still in his teens, and shared his ministry of healing. He later became a Catholic priest and founded, and remains president of, the Acton Institute for the Study of Religion and Liberty in 1990. Whenever Andre Crouch and the Disciples were in town they came to *The Catacombs* to minister the gospel through their music. Holy Hubert, the legendary Bay area street minister, came to Seattle frequently to minister on the street and at *The Catacombs*.

This was the beginning of a Jesus Movement! This was the birth of the JESUS PEOPLE ARMY!

CHAPTER SIXTEEN

SCHOOLS OPEN THEIR DOORS

In the prayer room every new Christian was asked to fill out a follow-up card. There stood their name and address and telephone number. After some time we were able to see, "Oh, there are a lot of youth from Capitol Hill. Yes, there are a lot of believers in the University district! Wow, look, there are a lot of followers from Queen Anne Hill." From this, we were able to put all the believers in one area together to form a "cell" for Jesus in their school. The school authorities gave the youth of their city a classroom to meet in once a week for prayer and fellowship. This, of course, resulted in more and more youth deciding for Jesus. We often heard, "Where shall we go this week-end?" It was the word around town, "Why we're going to the Catacombs across from the Space Needle." And so they did!

Every single weekend the Catacombs was packed with Seattle's youth. Not only were the numbers of believers growing, but the number of disciples or full-time workers was growing too. Two houses (the House of Esther and the House of Caleb) soon became four, adding a House of Rachel for the girls and a House of Joshua for the boys. We were also growing in the knowledge of God. We loved God's Word, the Bible. In fact, I not only taught the full-time workers from the Bible, but the Jesus People would carry their Bibles with them everywhere they went. When there was free time, you would see them learning from the Bible. The key questions were, "What did Jesus say? What did Jesus do?" When a situation would come up, they would ask, "What would Jesus do?"

The success and power present in *The Catacombs* caused an explosion of coffee houses in the towns all around Seattle. Not only did more and more high schools have Christians meeting weekly for prayer and sharing, but high schools and junior high schools began to ask me to come and speak in their school assemblies. It was hard to keep the attention of hundreds in a student body. But God helped me, and the students loved me. These doors kept opening and helped keep *The Catacombs* packed!

CHAPTER SEVENTEEN

LIVING IN HELL

The speech I gave in Seattle's high schools went like this:

"Don't you dare preach to me about hell—that's what I am living in right now. I want to take you to a life where people are living like animals: the misery of a drug addict.

You can find them in a shooting gallery, or up on the top of a roof, or in some dingy basement sticking a needle in their arm. They put the tourniquet around their arm until the vein in their arm protrudes. Then they take a cooker consisting of a bottle cap held by a hairpin. Four portions of water and one of heroin. They then boil this solution.

They take a long gory needle like the kind the nurse sticks in you and stick it into their protruding vein. It goes straight to their heart to give them what they call their "rush" or their "high."

I'll never forget the cry of a doper named Maria. You may have read about Maria and me in the book, *The Cross and the Switchblade*, by David Wilkerson. She said, "Linda, there is no way out for me except a life time term in jail, or to commit suicide, or to die of an overdose," in which your body swells up twice its size and becomes the color of charcoal.

I walked into the scene of a guy with a habit of 75 dollars a day. He cracked a raw egg, put it into a cup and drank it down. I said to him, "Listen, is this the only life you can find?"

He said, "Linda, when you're behind dope like a dope fiend, you don't have the natural appetites for food, or sex drive. I have to eat three raw eggs a day in order to survive. I have to drink these ol' vitamin pills."

I'll never forget their stories. It seems to happen to them all the same way. They want you to have a blast. They want you to have a party. They give you the dope the first time for free. It takes one to three shots before you are hooked. That means, you've got to have it. You can't live without it!

At the beginning you may be living rather nicely. You may have a job. You may have a pretty wife and kids. Everything seems to be going great for you. But, the stories are all the same. You can't really get going for the day without your dope. Though you may start out with a job, you can't continue to hold it down, because you've got to have a fix and easy money. You can't be waiting for your pay check to arrive every Friday, so you find you have to hustle every day to get your money. You have to mug somebody on the street, break into someone's home. As it becomes closer to the time you need another shot you become careless. You don't know if the police are going to pick you up or not. You have a fear deep inside you, a fear of being hunted down like an animal. The feds are watching for you around every corner. As soon as you meet a connection, there is even a greater fear, because maybe someone will jump you, put a knife to your throat and push you up against a wall, take your dope or even leave you dead. There is always the fear of the dope pusher, who may give you milk sugar instead of the real thing.

Before long your life is like that of an animal. Your friends and family are all gone and the only thing happening is, "When can I get my next shot?" If you were not able to get that, you may be forced to go home and get your own television and take it to the pawn shop. You plan to get your television back as soon as you get some extra money, but that does not happen as you also pawned your radio, your shaver, etc. Your home soon comes down to nothing. You have to take other peoples' things. You apologize to your wife, but she decides to go. One by one the friends are gone. You find yourself alone and sick. You can't see the sun and beautiful stars. You only dream of mountains and mountains of "snow" (heroin). You share a shot using a dirty needle. It is full of hepatitis or AIDS. You end up roaming the streets, not able to sleep or eat. You're living a life of hell.

CHAPTER EIGHTEEN

THE MONKEY STORY

SPEECH CONTINUED

"Heroin is like a cute little monkey," I said. "It happens like this: You're walking home from school one day. The cutest little monkey comes up to you and says, "Hey, baby, you sure are looking good. Let me hold your hand." You laugh at him right in the face, "I am in the top of my class, in the top of my society, and I have a good family. I have been taught not to hold hands with a monkey."

The next day you are coming home from school again, and would you believe it, that cute monkey is there again, looking you right in the face. He says, "Let me hold your hand." In fact, he is there every day. The first few times you tell him where to get lost. But after a while, he starts to eat your mind till you start having visions of this monkey.

Then one day you just feel like the devil. You say, "Today I feel like doing something groovy." You just break down and hold the hand of that monkey. At first you look all around, you're rather scared, you say, "Yikes, I hope nobody sees me."

The next day the monkey is there and asks if he can hold your hand again. You answer, "Of course not." But, a few days later you break down again and hold his hand. And, so it becomes that you hold the hands of that monkey every day. You don't care after a while who even sees you.

Time passes by and one day the monkey says, "You know, you are so irresistible, I've just got to have more of you. How about letting me jump up and swing on your arm?" And you reply, "You're kidding! Why it would be a long day in May, before I'd ever let you do that." But the monkey keeps asking to ride on the arm, until one day you say, "Okay."

However, after riding on the arm, one day the monkey just jumps up on your shoulder. You are a little nervous, but let it go. Then the monkey says, "I'll only ask for one more thing. Let me ride on your back." You give in, thinking at least you won't have to see him.

All of a sudden he cries out, "Help, help, help!"

"What's wrong with you?" you ask.

"I'm falling off," the monkey says, and with that he puts his hands around your neck and holds on tighter and tighter. Make no mistake he knows how to choke you to death! You see, he doesn't care what happens to you, whether you are found in an alley dead from an overdose, or whether you've gotten a life-long sentence in jail.

Let me tell you, that's the way it goes. It starts with just the little things. They have been asking me all across America, "What is wrong with LSD? What is wrong with blowing a little weed. Tell me, Linda, can you tell me that?" Now, I'm going to tell you plain like it is. Marijuana? Did you know that 90 to 95% of all hard dopers started by smoking Marijuana? You say, "Linda, that won't happen to me. That's what they all say. You think you are different and so tough?"

The Voice

CHAPTER NINETEEN

METH

Let me tell you what more happens when you use marijuana. The first thing it does is break down your fear. It eats your mind just like that monkey. That big wall you had, to stay away from drugs, is now broken down. You're not afraid of drugs anymore.

The second thing it does, is place you in a drug- oriented crowd. Whenever you find someone who is using pot, there's someone in that crowd who is using something more. Someone is using speed. Someone is taking trips on LSD. Someone is taking ecstasy pills, cocaine, heroin, or even meth. You can begin to think that the marijuana is just an old drag. Just then one of these new friends will say, "If you want to know what is really swinging try this." If you give in once, don't tell me you won't give in again.

I just read a very shocking report. It states that Meth use is now the USA's top drug problem, followed by cocaine (19%), marijuana (17%), heroin (3%). ("Meth Abuse Cited as Top Drug Problem for Law Enforcement Agencies", *Associated Press*, July 6, 2005) Methamphetamine, or Meth as it is called, is clinically recognized as the most destructive drug yet. The return-to-use rate for heroin and crack cocaine after using it twice is 20%. The return-to-use rate for Meth after using it twice is as high as 95%. Meth addiction is a recognized disease by the U.S. medical profession. The US Meth problem is presently growing the fastest in the upper Midwest, Southwest, and the Northwest. There has been a 93% increase in meth-related arrests.

One day in Seattle I met a really big Biker-looking type with bushy, red hair, and a heavy beard. He towered over me, nearly like David and Goliath. He had on a big, black leather coat. I began to tell him how much Jesus loved him. "Are you really happy inside?" I asked. As I continued to share with him, tears began to run down his cheeks, and then he was crying like a baby. "Oh, Linda," he said. "God couldn't possibly want me. I have made LSD in my bathtub at home and sold it to young people throughout Washington. I have been a biker and hurt lots of people. I've done criminal things. There's no hope for me." I prayed for Tiny. The Holy Spirit was faithful to comfort him and help him to believe that Jesus' blood shed on the cross was powerful enough to wash all his sins away. "If we confess our sins, He is faithful and just to forgive us *our* sins, and to cleanse us from all unrighteousness." (1 John 1:9)

Tiny had a real experience with Jesus that day. In the days to follow he boldly stood in front of young people in the streets, parks, coffee houses, or out-reaches to tell his story of how Jesus had truly given him a new beginning! In the Jesus Movement 400 Hells Angels from California turned on to Jesus and began to preach Him.

The Voice

CHAPTER TWENTY

SPIRITUAL REVOLUTION

In 1969, Woodinville, Washington, was the site of a huge Rock Festival to which thousands of youth came. We Jesus People went to this festival with thousands of flyers and witnessed to hundreds of youth! Later we also held our own Festival for Jesus in Seattle's Volunteer Park!

Greater Seattle Inc. sponsored a pop festival for its youth at Gold Creek Park. The Saturday night of this festival, a King County Sheriff officer reported to us that there were an estimated 25,000 young people at the festival.

He said there had been a barrage of calls from irritated neighbors, as well as from frantic parents reporting teenage runaways. Young people were taking drugs and participating openly in all types of sexual acts. Everywhere signs were openly advertising "Get your LSD, Marijuana, and Speed here." Communist literature was being widely distributed. Acres and acres of flesh reminded one of a modern day Sodom and Gomorrah.

This scene was a great challenge to us as we looked upon it. By this time, we were not just workers who helped bring the message of Jesus in the summer, but had actually become a Jesus People Army just like I had seen in the vision.

As the Jesus People Army went to prayer about the 25,000 youth at this festival, we got a bright idea. Why not rent an airplane and load it with our *Agape* newspaper, then fly low over the festival grounds dropping newspapers? That is exactly what we did! We flew the plane back and forth with a constant supply of *Agape* newspapers floating down into the reach of youth who desperately needed its message!

During Easter 1970, an ecumenical team consisting of leaders from every denomination, as well as the Jesus People Army, organized the "Spiritual Revolution" in the Seattle Center Ice Arena. Climaxing the three-day event was a Jesus March from the Ice Arena to the

Westlake Mall. The parade, held under a city permit and with police escort, started at 2.30 pm at the Civic Ice Arena. It streamed down 5th Avenue to Pine Street, west to 4th Avenue, and back to the Arena.

More than 3000 young adults attended this happening. I remember this march! Cars stopped by the police, TV-cameras focused on us, our innumerable signs, and banners shouting our message! I was marching in the lead together with Jim Palosaari and Bud Mowgli. We filled up the street as we walked with our banners and signs about Jesus!

Across the entire front of the parade stretched a banner reading "Spiritual Revolution." Signs carried by individuals read "Wise Men Shall Seek Him," "Let Sin Die," "He Lives", "Christ is the Answer," "Jesus is a Soul Man," and "God wants you." On a truck bed several youth were carrying a huge, heavy wooden cross. Overhead, a Piper Cruiser piloted by Art J. Bell of the Bell Air Service at Boeing Field spelled out in skywriting "Jesus Lives," and formed a huge cross in the sky. The marchers cheered, sang, and raised their arms in joy. It was truly an awesome event!

The Voice

CHAPTER TWENTY-ONE

THE NEXT BEST THING

I remember well that night at the Arena. A big guy walked up to me and boasted, "I am an atheist. You don't catch me believing in no God."

"That's no problem," I said, "But may I just pray for you? Now, when I pray you will feel a power touch your body. That's God. You'll then know He's real. If you feel Him, will you receive Him?"

"Yeah," he muttered. I prayed.

He exclaimed, "I've got it! Jesus I receive you now!"

Louis B. St. Cyr who attended this event in the Seattle Ice Arena, explains:

"I was born and raised a Roman Catholic. I was raised in a Catholic elementary school, Catholic high school, Catholic University. I studied out of Xavier University in New Orleans, Louisiana as a math and physics major. I changed from math and physics to electronic engineering in Los Angeles, Calif. I worked in the field of electronics for approximately thirteen years, simultaneously becoming an alcoholic and a doper. I have been into something of every scene. I have handled a lot of it. I was into the militant scene for a while. I was also in quite a few jails across the country. God started dealing with my life. I left the militant scene in 1969.

"One day when I was in Wyoming, some brothers picked me up and gave me a ride to Portland. I had no real reason to be in Portland. I would go back to San Francisco or maybe up to Seattle. I went to Seattle and that is where God got me. Of course, I did not know this at the time. I had been in Seattle for a few days. I went to a movie to see a documentary of Martin Luther King. I came out of the movie more up tight than ever, to be greeted by some hippie types passing out some flyers advertising a march for Jesus. I looked at the person who gave it to me, and just said to myself and to my partner, "Wow, these hippies have got a brand new bag," and I just walked away from them. But a few days later, I was in downtown

Seattle getting high and a couple of people approached me with Bibles in their hands. I saw them coming and right away my defenses went up. One of them said, "Brother, can we talk to you?" I said, "No." So he said, "Okay, brother, we'll talk to you later." I said, "Yeah, later." They went away. But they came back later and said, "Brother, remember us?" Before I knew it, one of them had me by the arm, my booze still in one hand, led me to their car, and they drove away with me. I didn't care, I could have cared less. It was just a matter of relocating, 'cause I knew I could get high on one side of town just as easy as the other.

"I arrived at Seattle Center at an Arena they have there. Right away I saw it was a revival. I sat there and listened to them and the thing that caught my eye was the Roman Catholic Priest who got up to speak. I listened to him and after he finished speaking, I went back and spoke to him for a while. Somehow, without me ever intending it, I went right up there and got prayed for, and later that day I ended up in a Christian commune called "The House of Joshua." Being as rebellious as I had been all my life, and with as much hatred I had in my heart, it was kinda hard for me to really accept Jesus Christ. So I had to sit around and watch the Christians for a while just to try and figure out what was happening, because it really freaked me out. I sat around for three days, afraid to eat anything because I was suspicious of that many people being happy all the time. I had just seen quite a few riots, I had seen quite a bit of rebellion throughout the world, and I had prepared to do the next best thing. And when I finally realized the reality of Jesus Christ, I wanted all that I could get. All that He had to offer. I finally gave in to Him. I thank Him for choosing me, because I do not deserve to be his servant, having been so wrong all my life. Something I haven't had is compassion. I thank God for giving that to me!"

CHAPTER TWENTY–TWO

PUBLIC BAPTISMS

By now there were literally hundreds who needed to be baptized. What could I do? Clearly we would baptize them outdoors in water around Seattle! Green Lake was one perfect place! Crowds would gather around us, also media, as we met. I would explain the meaning of water baptism. It is a symbol that our old man with his old nature is dead as one was put under the water, and that as one came up out of the water he was "a new man in Christ, with old things passed away and all things becoming new!

Doug Parris explains:

"I was there at Green Lake for one of the mass baptisms. Baptized as an infant, I asked the advice of Dennis Bennet, famed Episcopal priest of Saint Luke's in Ballard, if I should also be baptized as a believer. He thought so, and I waited until the Green Lake outreach and was baptized with the new converts. My confession before they dunked me was an evangelistic message there in a very public place. Since then I've believed in the strategic value of public baptisms."

The Jesus People Army that until now had mainly impacted Seattle and surrounding areas was about to expand into the entire Pacific Northwest. This was a consequence of more and more young radical youth getting a burden for the entire region.

Jim Palosaari explained:

"In the late '60s I was involved in the riots at San Francisco and at People's Park in Berkley. While tending a "head" bar, I lived in the Haight-Ashbury district and saw a lot of rip-offs, burnings, and just pure apathy as the flower children began to wilt.

After rejecting the Haight-Ashbury scene, (I lived with the greatest flamenco guitar players, the greatest actors, the greatest singers. We all were so busy being great in there, we were afraid to come out), I headed for Canada. One late afternoon as we were traveling, I had been drinking and my girl, Sue, was on my back about it, because I was spending all the money for the trip. She said she was going to leave me. That shook me up. She had never said that before. My life passed before me. I jumped out of the van and raised my hands. "I quit," I shouted. "I give up!" I didn't even know who I was quitting or what I was giving up." But, God saw that Jim was ready to die. It was my spiritual Waterloo. My girl apologized. She had never seen me give up before and it scared her.

We drove on and within an hour we saw a sign: Cathcart Tent Revival. It was as though God had said, "He's quit. Now I can work on him." We drove up to the revival because it had camping facilities, but when we went into the tent the Holy Spirit came upon us. They said we were experiencing Jesus. We didn't know who Jesus was, but we sure were experiencing something. We kept returning and on the fifth night we gave our lives to Christ."

A short time after this, Jim and Sue Palosaari joined the Jesus People Army in Seattle. There I taught them the Word and trained them under my ministry. Later, Jim became my coordinator for the JPA. He was truly another one of God's front-line fighters for Jesus.

One day as Jim and Sue and I were sharing, Jim said, "Linda, I think it is time for us to expand to other cities." Earnest prayer was made about this, and the answer we received from the LORD was a green light. The cities that the Jesus People Army would invade for Jesus were: Spokane, Yakima, Boise, Vancouver, and Edmonds.

CHAPTER TWENTY–THREE

SPOKANE

We made the plan. We secured permission to hold an outreach in Spokane's Highbridge Park and at Shadle Park Bowl. A pastor friend arranged a place for the Jesus Army to sleep. We were given a storefront to use as our witnessing base for the Outreach. Little did we know that right around the corner from where we were, there was a coffee house where the youth hung out. This was no ordinary coffee house. Their life style was one of drugs, free sex, alcohol, and some were into cults and witchcraft. You might call it the devil's coffee house, or the devil's headquarters. From there they produced an underground newspaper for Spokane with their messages. They even had their own band, The Wilson-McKinley.

When we arrived in Highbridge Park, we found it full of young people turning on to sex, drugs, and alcohol. We had advertised ourselves as "Jesus People Music Concert." Since we had no stage, we pulled several park benches together. Different Jesus People sang and testified. I jumped up on the park bench and spoke. My speech went something like this:

"I challenge you to take a second and think about God. God loves you, and He sees exactly how things are going or not going for you. Drugs and drunkeness are only an attempt to escape from reality. They cannot truly satisfy. The missing piece is God. The emptiness you are feeling can only be filled with God. I challenge you to try our Jesus. The Bible says, 'whosoever shall call on the name of the LORD shall be saved.' Who in this park will be brave enough to walk up in front of this park bench and say, 'I need God in my life.'

It was then that the Holy Spirit took over. He could be felt in that park. After I'd spoken, I asked who in the park would make the decision to receive Jesus. To my surprise, about half of the youth raised their hands. I thought there must be a misunderstanding, so I repeated myself, "Who here in this park wants to decide now to receive Jesus?" This time even more hands went up. In fact two-thirds of the youth came down and knelt in front of the park bench I was standing on. They prayed the sinner's prayer and gave Jesus their lives. That afternoon we were baptizing new converts for two solid hours in the nearby river. One young man threw 250 dollars worth of acid in the river (that would be $1,479 in 2012 dollars). Another man threw an ounce of heroin in the water. The next day we baptized new converts for two more hours. By then over 350 Spokane youth had been saved.

As we began to pray with them, they would begin to cry. They asked Jesus into their life, and all the time, more and more youth came forward. We would invite the new believers back to our storefront. There we shared with them from our Bibles and talked into the morning hours. The next day, young people kept coming by our storefront. That night in the park, even more came. Our band played, our soldiers testified, and I preached. The conviction of the Holy Spirit came across the park. When I invited youth to turn on to God they came from every corner of the park. The youth prayed and wept. The next day, youth from the devil's coffee house began to come over to us. Right there in broad day light some of the heaviest dopers prayed for God's salvation!

That night in the park new believers stood on the benches and told their story, "This is real. Jesus has forgiven my sins! I know God is in me, and I am so Happy!"

The end result of our visit to Spokane was that so many youth from there got Jesus, that the devil's club closed down. Their ungodly newspaper closed down. Their band Wilson-McKinley got salvation, and decided to play only for Jesus. Seven houses opened up for the new believers who wanted to now work for Jesus. The Spokane youth opened a Jesus People *I Am* coffee house on Main and Browne. The majority of the youth of Spokane were now Christians!

Sue Palosaari Cowper explains:

"It was you, Linda, who instigated that day when hundreds were baptized down at the river. I was there. I remember one day, when all the hippies were lying around on the grass smoking weed, and I came up to you and told you they needed to hear the message of salvation. I remember you got up on a picnic table and told them you'd be coming back the next day with a message that would change their life. Lou, Jim, and I were there. You came back the next day with a flat bed truck, the choir sang, Jim, Lou, and Tiny gave their testimony, and then you preached. After that you told them they needed to get saved, and then you told them the next step was to be baptized in water. They lined up and all of them followed you down to the river. It was a miraculous happening!"

CHAPTER TWENTY–FOUR

BOISE

From Spokane the JPA were booked in Julia Davis Park in Boise, Idaho. A kind pastor fixed places for us to stay. However, now we were not just the JPA members from Seattle. The Wilson-McKinley band asked if they could go with us and sing for Jesus, and scores of new believers from Spokane asked if they, too, could go with us to help share the good news. Of course, we said yes. So, Boise experienced a real invasion!

I'll never forget that night on the stage when I was speaking to the Boise youth. I felt the power of God. I challenged the dark powers to let go of the youth. The D's had to Go! The devil and demons, the drugs, the drunkenness, the darkness and depressions and divisions. I asked for a barrel to be brought up by the stage. Then I challenged Boise youth to walk up front and throw their devilish things in that barrel to burn and then to come stand in front of me for the salvation prayer. And, the youth came. They threw their dope, occult magazines, nude pictures, cigarettes, etc. into the fire burning in that barrel! What a Fire!

They stood before me and we prayed together. Jesus washed them clean and came into their lives. They felt the joy of being with God. This hit state and national press, including Associated Press, as $2000 ($11,842 in 2012) worth of drugs burned. CBS Television also sent word that they wanted to film this tremendous event. Over 700 young people became Christians. A house was established in Boise called *The Stone House*. *TIME* Magazine published an article about these meetings in their August 3, 1970 issue. The city was never the same.

CHAPTER TWENTY-FIVE

YAKIMA

Then we all converged on Yakima. Seattle, Spokane, and Boise youth came to spread the good news of Jesus with this city, that also fell under the presence of the Spirit of God, and its youth became Christians! The newspaper headline read, "Holy Spirit Falls on Yakima Valley."

Jesus People seemed to be coming in from every direction. Everywhere you turned, you would run into a "Jesus Freak" or two or three or four or five, even before the revival was to begin.

The Wilson-McKinley had been playing in the high schools two days prior to the meetings, priming their hearts and letting them know that Jesus loved them and wanted them to live only for him. Apparently, Jesus must have been talking to them, for they came to the meeting in large numbers, all three nights.

The scene happened at George Washington Junior High School Auditorium. I called for soldiers for Christ, asking, "Which side will you choose?" The Wilson-McKinley played, their music nearly shaking loose the light fixtures and many Jesus People proclaimed with zeal what Jesus had done in their lives. After all the music, and after all the speaking, I gave an altar call. "Who, this night, would like to give his or her life to Jesus?" The Spirit of God filled the auditorium and 21 people came forward to receive Jesus. An altar call was given the second night. The Spirit of God came. There were twice as many people who received Jesus.

The third night arrived. It was Saturday and many young people were there, either out of curiosity or by invitation from a friend or one of the Jesus People. The altar call was given. Wow! They came forward, one by one, two by two, five by five... they just kept coming. It was so fantastic I lost count! They sold out to Jesus Christ!

Their coffee house was called the *JP House* at 617 West Yakima Ave.

Yakima

Cheryl Estep, a JPA member from Yakima, was one of the main sources of strength in this revival. The Jesus House was called the House of Elijah. The first house was on 16th Avenue and was established in 1970 according to Cheryl. She shares:

"Linda asked me to stay in Yakima after the revival and start a Jesus House, since I was from Yakima. We got a house with no furniture. Linda said we had been talking about living by faith, so this was a chance to practice it. Our little team cleaned the house every day, and we stayed in homes of people from the church. We made a list of all the things we needed for the house. I remember thinking, 'I do not have any way to get this furniture.' I remembered a sermon, which said to thank God for the things ahead of time. So, we went down the list and thanked God for everything on it. That week people began to bring to the house the things we needed, which were on the list. By the end of the week we had everything, except the refrigerator. By the next week we had a 'fridge! This was so exciting to see God do it!"

The Voice

CHAPTER TWENTY–SIX

VANCOUVER

The next city on our calendar was Vancouver, British Columbia. This was the first international break-through for the Jesus People Army. We conducted a weeklong revival in the Pender Auditorium in Vancouver, where numerous people (mostly acid heads) gave their lives to Jesus, but not without a struggle.

First, we had to contend with the border guards. There were three rules for entry into Canada: 1. Everyone had to be over 18 years old. 2. No one could have a police record. 3. Convicted dope users couldn't cross.

So, there you have it: about 150 Jesus People and these rules eliminated about 90% of us. We dispersed and tried another entry at Blaine, Washington, and still no luck. We then went back to the original crossing and camped there. Finally, by going through in separate car and on foot, we made it into Canada, and we were on our way to Vancouver.

To the eye it was a beautiful city. However, in the spirit it was depressing. The whole city seemed to reek with hate, lust, greed, idolatry, witchcraft, and every other fruit of sin, more than any city we had encountered so far. The estimate was that there were 50,000 acid-heads in this city. The city was hard. One of our men was beat up in an alley and another one of our girls had her Bible grabbed out of her hand and torn up. I saw young girls who were on smack holding their stomachs in pain from using the drugs and begging at the same time for money to get more.

The JPA held our Pender Auditorium revival there (in the Gas Town section of the city) every night for a week. After the first four nights the people were beginning to discover the reality of what Jesus was trying to do. Especially after we stuck it out in spite of the threats, the jeering, and the opposition in general. The Spirit of the LORD did give us a break-through there.

There were over 150 youth from the street and drug scene that got saved. It was enough to cause us to obtain three Jesus Houses with full-time disciples. They held Bible studies every week Wednesday through Sunday at 1020 Main Street.

The Associated Press reporter wrote:

"Testimonies, rock songs with religious lyrics, Jesus power buttons, and a lot of Praise the LORD combined to draw several hundred Vancouver young people to the first JPA meeting here on Wednesday. About 50 of the army arrived last week, and already have been given a house for a commune and a vacant coffee house. They have published their own paper and have ambitious plans for the future. Jim Palosaari, Pacific Northwest coordinator of the JPA, stepped out on the stage and surveyed the hundreds of youth in the crowd saying, "You can just call us Jesus freaks if you want to." Russ Griggs then led every one in "Give me that old time religion." The "Vision" band from Seattle belted out three more songs. Then came testimonials. First, it was Tiny. With polished delivery he boomed his story into the mic and mesmerized the audience. That was the pattern for the meeting. There were four more songs and then a testimony from a former black militant. Linda Meissner from the pages of The Cross and the Switchblade preached. When the call came to accept Jesus, 25 came forward. Out-side the auditorium 15 more youth said yes to Jesus."

Bill Ireland explains:

"I was in Seattle/Tacoma when Linda Meissner and the Jesus People Army were in full flower in 1971. I lived communally in JPA in Vancouver, B.C. that year. It was a time of great revival like none I have ever seen before or since. Christian Rock bands sprung up out of nowhere. There were Christian coffee houses everywhere, and concerts with an incredible profusion of talent. One night at a coffee house in Vancouver, we danced before the LORD till the fire department came and told us to "knock it off." They were afraid the floor was going to collapse."

CHAPTER TWENTY-SEVEN

EDMONTON

While the JPA continued on to Seattle, I decided to swing by Edmonton, Alberta on the way. I quickly formed a small team from the believers in the town, and together we began sharing the gospel with unbelievers. We rented a high school auditorium to hold rallies in. We also went to several parks. Soon the newspapers started writing about us. Then came the time to start a coffee house and some commune houses for the JPA. We got a building and named it *The Fishing Hole Coffee House*. This was the scene for many of the meetings in the Edmonton outreach.

During one of the first nights there as I was walking through a park, a guy came running up to me, grabbed me, and started crying, "I'm in the wrong boat!" Immediately I started praying that he would enter into the Gospel ship. He did and was filled with the Holy Spirit right there in the park.

Later that night I was speaking in a church, and he came in with five of his friends. By the end of the night, three of them were saved and baptized in the Holy Spirit. It turned out that he was one of the main dope dealers in the town. He had a crash pad where people would come every night and pick up their dope. After the meeting I went there with him. His girl was there and within a few minutes she got saved. Then three more came and they got saved!

Well, this little group of new believers started a Bible study in this crash pad. During the Bible study one night, two big guys walked in and noticed two guys reading Bibles. This really got them up tight and one started cursing and said, "I'm going into the living room where the freaks are." So, they walked into the living room to find 25 to 30 Jesus Freaks studying their Bibles. They said, "Sit down, God is really talking to us out of this book." They sat down and listened!

This kind of thing was happening all over! Heads were turning on to Jesus. It was not because of Linda Meissner or the JPA; it was because the Holy Spirit was now starting to be poured out just like the Bible said it would, "And it shall come to pass in the last days, says God, That I will pour out of my Spirit on all flesh" (Acts 2:17).

The revival continued to spread to all the cities across the Pacific Northwest, with many more miracles and multitudes turning to Jesus Christ, following the same pattern as the stories I have shared above. Literally tens of thousands of lives were changed as Jesus ignited the hearts of an entire generation.

The Voice

CHAPTER TWENTY-EIGHT

BACK TO SEATTLE

In the summer of 1971, we decided to make a strategic revival outreach in Seattle, this time with many new believers from cities throughout the Pacific Northwest who had been hit by the revival and were now part of the Jesus People Army.

A JPA disciple explains:

"As I stepped out of the car I could feel the excitement in the air. The streets were lined with people with their faces reflecting looks of joy, some with bewilderment and even some looks of anger as they tried to figure out just exactly what was happening. Probing through the curious crowd it brought to mind the atmosphere of a Rock Festival, the heavy music, the bright clothing, abundance of hair, but instead of the sweet smell of marijuana filling the air, it was the Spirit of God. This was the beginning of the first night of the five-day Seattle revival at the Moore Theater."

"Months of planning had gone into this event. And, now it had become a reality. Jesus Freaks from all over the Northwest and Canada came to help turn Seattle on to Jesus. Christ said in the last days before His coming, that He would pour out His spirit upon the hippies and the dopers, because the people who were invited in the first place would be too busy to serve Him. He said He would invite people into His kingdom, the bad and the good (Matthew 22:10) and you can see it come to pass right before your eyes. Each night of the five day meeting became heavier and heavier. People dropping to their knees, turning away from dope, asking Jesus into their hearts, and giving their lives to Christ. People were sincerely dedicating their lives to spreading the good news of Jesus Christ.

"The LORD said in the last days He would raise up an army to preach His word, and this Seattle revival was an example of that part of Scripture coming to pass. During the day before the meetings the streets of Seattle were invaded by literally hundreds of Christ's disciples. Every inch of the city was covered, not one stone was left unturned. Each person heard the Gospel preached, not only by those who were old in the Lord, but also by those who had just received the fresh clean life giving Spirit of God only the night before. There's nothing more beautiful than seeing someone who is only a few hours old in the Lord sincerely sharing their experience with those who haven't met Christ. You don't have to go to Bible school to explain the simplicity of just opening up your heart and letting Jesus in. Something so simple, but so important, that's what it is all about. Just sharing the most beautiful experience in the world with others. I don't think Seattle will be quite the same. From now on its streets will be alive with the voice of the Lord speaking the message of the Kingdom soon to come.

"Andre Crouch and the Disciples headlined the first night of the revival with the Wilson-McKinley and The Glorious Liberty. Each group expressed the good news of Jesus Christ through their music. I am sure that a lot of the heads living in Seattle were surprised to see one of their old friends up on the stage. His name is Tiny. At one time he belonged to an organization that produced most of the dope that was run through the Northwest. He's an ex-biker who at one time would just as soon stomp you as look at you. Now he has so much love pouring through him it's hard to believe it's the same guy. He has devoted his life to the preaching of God's word. Linda Meissner spoke to us of the vision that we all must have, and that is to go into all the world and teach the Gospel to every creature, and it will be done. After five days of witnessing, learning, music, and 500 souls brought to the Lord it came time to baptize the new Christians. Green Lake, located north of Seattle, was chosen as the place where the baptism was to be held. Great crowds gathered to watch, as many of the new converts were submerged in the cold water on that brisk November day. A baptism is an outward confession of dedicating your life to Jesus Christ, and the people on that day must have been sincere about it, to allow themselves to be dunked into that cold water."

We had only booked five days of meetings, but the outpouring just continued. We continued meeting every night in the Catacombs, where young youth just kept coming and surrendering their lives to Jesus.

CHAPTER TWENTY-NINE

JESUS PEOPLE MOVEMENT

While revival was taking place all across the cities of the Pacific Northwest, God was getting ready to do the same all across the country.

He had already poured out His spirit in California. In Southern California there was Chuck Smith of Calvary chapel and others. In Berkley there was Jack Sparks. There was Duane Pederson, also a leader in the Jesus Movement. He was the founder of the Hollywood Free Press, which had a distribution of 500,000 out on the streets of California. In fact, Duane was the first to coin the phrase, "Jesus People Movement."

One day Jim Palosaari met with me to share the burden he had on his heart for his hometown in Wisconsin. He said him and his wife, Sue, wanted to raise up a Jesus People Movement there. We prayed together about this and felt the green light to go ahead. This was exactly what Jesus had in mind. "And the things that thou hast heard of me among many witnesses, the same commit thou to Faithful men, who shall be able to teach others also." (2 Timothy 2:2). Jim invited me to Milwaukee to speak at the Milwaukee War Memorial for a Jesus People concert on February 1971.

Michael Drehfal explains, "I will never forget the night when we all were in the hallway just outside the meeting area, and you, Linda, prayed for us to receive the baptism in the Holy Spirit, and He fell on us all! I was overwhelmed with joy and spoke in tongues. I then joined the Milwaukee Jesus People."

Sue Palosaari Cowper shares, "Linda was in Milwaukee at least a month, speaking in home meetings, and different churches, as well as the rally. She was always the last one to turn out the lights, a tireless apostle who never left the building until all gathered there had been prayed for to receive the baptism in the Holy Spirit. Linda was very much the ground-well that became the Milwaukee Jesus People, still spreading its wings hither and yon."

The Milwaukee Jesus People later separated into three Jesus People branches. Jim and Sue took one team to Europe. One team became Jesus People USA based out of Chicago. Then one team joined Bill Lowery's tent ministry, *Christ is the Answer*.

By now, the Jesus People Movement was spreading like wildfire all across the U.S.A. Governor Ronald Reagan hailed the movement when he met with Pope Paul VI in 1969; "...so many young people had simply turned from drugs to a faith in Jesus." (Bob Slosser, *Reagan Inside Out*, 1984).

Likewise, David Wilkerson told Associated Press, reprinted in *The Seattle Times* October 24, 1970: "I see among these young people the beginnings of a righteousness revolution which will be the biggest thing that ever hit this country." He said of the youth subculture: "They are looking for a charismatic experience, for a spiritual source, and this is turning into a Jesus Movement. It is a genuine religious awakening and it is going on all over the country."

This was a true revival, and I wish I could say that my part in it continued until this day from glory to glory. Alas, now we reach a sad, but equally important part of my story. I share this so that you, the next generation, will avoid making the same mistakes that I did.

The Voice

CHAPTER THIRTY

CHILDREN OF GOD

CBS national television produced a documentary, aired on *60 Minutes*, about a Jesus group called Children of God. They presented a positive picture of this group living on their Texas ranch. It was so popular, that they showed it a second time. I did not see this film, but the Jesus People Army leader, Russ Griggs, of Vancouver, Canada, did. He was so impressed, that he shared what he saw with the other JPA leaders, including me. However, by the time he came down to Seattle to share with me personally, he had already decided to pull out of JPA and join COG. I was shocked. I decided I had to find out who these people were, so I drove to Los Angeles, where COG were based.

They were a big, strong, well-organized group. They had excellent music, organized Bible classes, and went witnessing every day. Everything I saw was impressive. I was glad to see what was seemingly another strong, on-fire Jesus People group. Of course, I was not glad that they would be taking my Jesus People Army from both Vancouver and Yakima, but I was going to make the best of it. So, when they informed me that they would be visiting Vancouver, I invited their music team to stop by our *Catacombs Coffee House* to perform on a Saturday night. There was nothing unusual about this, as I invited a different music group to play on stage every Friday and Saturday night. I had no idea we were in harm's way.

When the COG arrived, we thought they had come to perform on the stage. In reality, they had another agenda in mind: a hostile takeover of the Seattle JPA. From the moment they walked in our door, they took after us. They were organized in their plan. One COG member confronted each of us, one on one. They placed David Berg's daughter, Deborah, on me (David Berg was the leader of COG).

David had told his daughter to present herself as the leader of the COG, and Deborah introduced herself to me as such. Deborah was a young, charismatic, seemingly terrific leader in charge of what seemed to be an on fire Jesus movement. I was quite exited to talk with her. I was totally unprepared for what happened next.

With her Bible in hand she turned to Luke 14. Deborah declared that only those who "forsake *all*" were true disciples. She asked me the questions continually. Did I believe Jesus meant what he said in Luke 14:33, "Whoever of you does not forsake all that he has cannot be My disciple" And Mark 10:29, 30 "There is no one who has left house or brothers or sisters or father or mother or wife [husband] or children or lands, for My sake and the gospel's, who shall not receive a hundredfold now in this time —houses and brothers and sisters and mothers and children and lands, with persecutions— and in the age to come, eternal life." Did I love Jesus more than anything or anyone? Did I believe Jesus when he said, "Go therefore and make disciples of all nations, baptizing them... teaching them to observe all things that I have commanded you." (Matthew 28.19:20)

I was not prepared for this sort of confrontation. My honest answer to all of these questions was yes. JPA had taken the Gospel to the cities in our region, but I had felt that it was time for us to go to other nations of the world. In fact, I had been looking for a location to start a training center for disciples to prepare themselves to go to the nations of Europe. Deborah told me great visions of nations they were in, and how if I were only willing to forsake all, I could go and start preaching in them.

Deborah talked to me every day that followed, while they saw to it that we were not being interrupted by anyone else. The parallel to Jesus' temptation in the desert comes to mind, only I had no idea that this angel of light in front of me was systematically brainwashing me. Without knowing it, I was being deceived into thinking that the COG was the perfect next step for my ministry. I thought that by joining the COG I could fulfill my heart's cry to take the gospel to the nations.

They divided us the first night. Almost all my leadership from Seattle and Tacoma walked out at the end of a 12-hour meeting with their team, but the Seattle foot soldiers had gone to bed and woke to new leaders. Some of those decided to join the COG, while the majority did not.

CHAPTER THIRTY-ONE

EUROPE

The drama surrounding the split in the JPA caught the attention of the mass media. Soon they were reporting Linda Meissner had joined the Children Of God. The story finally got so hot that the news went national on Associated Press. This was more than COG could handle.

Deborah decided to fly me out of the United States. On the way to the plane, I was contacted by a delegation claiming to represent Ronald Reagan, then governor of California. Evidently, Reagan felt I was one of the leading youth leaders in America, and I was offered one million dollars and all the support I needed to stay and start a new youth work in America. Before I could really give them an answer, I was already on my way to catch my plane, disappearing from the American scene.

On the plane, I was trying to make sense of what had just happened. I had not left Seattle in an orderly manner. I seemed to have been driven, rather than led. Rushed, not rested. And worst of all, I had left my family and my sheep in confusion. I trusted that the strong leaders whom I had trained and discipled, would be well able to continue the work. After all, both Paul and Jesus left their sheep behind when they continued to the next harvest field. But I also realized that there was something wrong with the transition. I worried about the fate of the sheep I had left behind and in light of that, all my dreams about reaching the world with the gospel didn't seem to matter as much. With tears in my eyes, I asked the Lord to forgive me for any hurt I had caused, and entrusted them into His hands. The Lord comforted me and reassured me, that He was with me. The revival that had begun in Seattle would spread to Europe. "Other sheep have I also which are not of this fold. Them also must I bring." (John 10:16)

The plane landed in London. I was driven to the COG headquarters there. Actually, they treated me rather special. They wanted me to preach. But how could I preach, with a broken heart? I'd left my family and I'd left my "sheep." I had no idea what would happen to those

I dearly loved. I felt dead inside. They told me to speak, but how could I "sing the Lord's song in a strange land" (Psalm 137:4)? After some time, however, I received spiritual strength again. I started to preach again, first traveling in Scotland and Northern Ireland during the Civil War. Then I preached in other European countries and ended up in Norway, preaching in many churches. All this time, I was not aware that COG was a cult. As far as I was concerned, I had simply joined another group of the Jesus People Movement in Europe. The COG had gone to great lengths to keep any irregularities from my knowledge. I only saw the good side that they presented, and knew nothing about their sins. So, I continued preaching the gospel!

I traveled to Sweden to meet a possible editor for a new newspaper. One night as I was walking down a street in Stockholm, I saw a nightclub full of teenagers. I walked in. There were young people drunk and stoned lying all over the floor and hanging from tables and chairs. I began to walk through the bodies on the floor. All of a sudden a 14-year-old girl cried out, "Linda, I know who you are, you're an angel sent from God to help me." She had never seen me before. I took her by the hand and pulled her up. I told her how much Jesus loved her. I prayed for her, and took her home with me and helped her. That was Abigail. God used her to really touch my life. I spent days in prayer after that, crying out for God to touch other youth in Scandinavia like her.

The Voice

CHAPTER THIRTY-TWO

UTTERMOST PART
OF THE EARTH

A leader of Children Of God came to Copenhagen. I was invited to come, too. He called me to the side and said, "Linda, we are very busy in London and don't have the time to work here in the north as much as we'd like. We have decided to ask you to be the leader of Scandinavia."

At the time I felt it was a miracle and answer to my prayers. There were very few disciples in Scandinavia, and the ones there were poor and not well taken care of. God anointed me once again. It is a miraculous story of how God changed the lives of hundreds of young people in towns and cities throughout the Scandinavian nations. They experienced a real revival like we had experienced in the Pacific Northwest. I was their leader and shepherd, and they were truly saved and filled with the Holy Spirit. As far as doctrines and practices were concerned, I was continuing with the same message and doctrine I had always preached in New York, across the USA, and in the Pacific Northwest. I saw my work in Scandinavia as a continuation of my work in the Pacific Northwest. As Jesus had commanded to take the message, first to Jerusalem, then to Judea and Samaria, and then to the uttermost parts of the Earth, I believed that I had now gone from Seattle to the five surrounding cities and now to the uttermost parts of the earth.

CHAPTER THIRTY-THREE

FORNICATION AND ADULTERY

We did, of course, read what was called the "Mo Letters." These were writings from David Berg—the leader of COG —that came with lessons on a somewhat regular basis. I did not agree with every single word, but we were all busy with the ongoing revival here in Scandinavia, and did not feel that the letters interfered with what we were doing.

Eventually, though they had tried to hide it from me, rumors of David Berg's sinful lifestyle began to slip out, and finally reached me, in spite of COG's endeavor to keep me in the dark. I began to learn of practices and doctrines that were not in accordance with God's Word. The worst of these rumors concerned the leadership being involved in sexual sins. I was disturbed to learn that David Berg had been living with his secretary a long while. He then found good reasons or excuses to add more wives. To cover his sins, he introduced free love into the circle of his closest leaders. I was totally shocked when I heard these things! One day, a Mo letter came called "Flirty Fishes." It said that disciples were to flirt with the unbelieving and bring them into COG by that method. As further evidence, I was shown a picture with David drunk and surrounded by his women. This was in strong contrast to everything we had preached and taught in Scandinavia. Under my leadership there, no such immorality had been introduced. I was outraged and objected strongly to my sheep against all these heresies. I began warning and teaching my sheep that this was against the teachings of God's Word.

A short time after that, a new Mo letter came from David Berg ordering everyone in COG to believe in and have free sex. I told London that I would NOT go along with that, neither would I allow my sheep to do so. I was totally devastated and was crying out to God as to what to do in this situation. Should I lead a rebellion and take my sheep? But before I could act, I was called by David Berg to take the quickest plane to Rome. The leadership wanted to talk to me in person. Never in my life have I had such a horrifying experience, as they demanded that I believe in and teach the free sex love message. They reprimanded me in the harshest words and tones for my rebellious north. They then provided me with an apartment in Venice, Italy for me to think things over.

The Voice

CHAPTER THIRTY-FOUR

A PUBLIC APOLOGY

I didn't need to think! The Bible says, "The works of the flesh are these: Adultery (sex outside of a marriage), fornication (sex between people who are not married)... drunkenness... of which I tell you that they which do such things shall not inherit the Kingdom of God." (Galatians 5:19-21)

I realized that I had been in a cult of the worst sort! I ordered a train ticket to Copenhagen, Denmark and left the Children Of God immediately. I have not seen them since that day. I only pray and hope that my final warnings to my sheep about the malpractice and heresies of David Berg helped a significant number of them to leave the COG.

I have asked for and received forgiveness from all the people that I know and have been in contact with over these 40 years, for the ways in which I hurt them. However, I understand that because my former ministry touched the lives of so many people, there are still dear people whom I have not been able to apologize to. I wish to do that publicly here and now. If you are one who was in any way hurt by my wrong actions, I humbly ask you now to please forgive me totally, even as Jesus has. You are welcome to write me, if you have something on your heart. I am on Facebook. You can write a private message there or to linda_may7@hotmail.com.

While visiting Seattle in 1988, I received a telephone call from Deborah. It seems she wrote a book telling the truth about her father, David Berg. She was crying desperately during that phone call. She said, "Linda, I lied to you. If I had told you the truth about my father and the leadership around him that time I was with you in Seattle, I know you and Russ Griggs would never have joined the COG. The conviction of my sin is heavy upon me. I beg you to forgive me in Jesus' name and release me from this burden." Of course, I forgave her that day.

CHAPTER THIRTY-FIVE

THE OCCUPY MOVEMENT

In the 1970s there was a vacated Danish military base full of abandoned buildings almost in downtown Copenhagen. This place was free for the taking. Copenhagen youth simply climbed over the fence and took a building to live in. They occupied the entire military base and called the free town "Christiana."

Many of the occupiers were full of fresh dreams. They didn't believe that the traditional way of doing things had all the answers. They wanted to try some new experiments, and so they did. Some lived together in a collective. They established an alternative life style.

From nothing they created an alternative village with all that was needed: a grocery shop, vegetable shop, shops with home-made hand work of various kinds, kindergarten, cafes, bath house, etc.

About 1000 youth ended up living there, plus the visitors from all over Denmark coming to visit what they had made. The Danish government followed the development there, and had documented that this "social experiment," as they called it, was having a positive result for many youth who could not actually fit into university or in a 9 to 5 job.

However, since there were so many people in this location, it attracted drug pushers to sell their wares on what became known as "Pusher Street." This caused fights with the police, and eventually destroyed the utopian dream. This was the perfect place for me to continue my missionary work for Jesus. I loved the youth. I loved souls. So I occupied a house there and started to work for God.

I married a blonde, blue eyed, Danish Viking I had met and won to the Lord a year before. We worked together in Christiania. In March 1977 I gave birth to a little baby boy. We named him Dan. Here is how he remembers those years.

Dan explains, "Being born into this world was like a newborn swallow being hurdled into a mighty storm, with only a small pair of wings to carry me, the wind pushing me to every side and with no sense of direction. No anchor, no lighthouse, no shielding place of protection. All around was noise, unrest and absence of peace. Yet, through this dark chaos I could feel my heart beating; a persevering pulse of hope like a voice in the darkness calling me towards the light.

I was born in 1977 in an abandoned military base that had been occupied by hippies, called Christiania. I remember daily clashes between police with truncheons and stone-throwing occupants. Dogs barking, whistling, screaming and shouting, rage and fear, and a very real sensation of a struggle between good and evil, righteousness and unrighteousness. Of course, in the naivety of a child's mind, it was the police that were the evildoers with their daily raids against Christiania.

Thus at an early age a clear black and white picture of the world was formed. A twisted picture in many ways, because I called good evil and evil good. But there remained an invisible link to the heavenly realm, that imbued me with a persistent joy, zeal, and energy, that like a laser-beam shot through my vivid fears and confusion. Thus it is, that in spite of how I felt, most people knew me as a happy and energetic little boy.

In those preschool years I had my first date with God. I remember sitting in a swing by myself, when suddenly I was caught up to another realm. Everything around me seemed to disappear and I felt so alone, as if I did not at all belong in this world. Tears flowed like rivers. I was desperately frightened and lonely.

Suddenly I felt a presence of something. Now I know it was God. At once I knew that I belonged in this world, that everything would turn out beautiful, and light would shine on me. Shortly after, I recognized the same presence as I watched a movie about Jesus, and I decided to surrender my life to Him. This changed everything! From now on, though darkness surrounded me, I was wrapped in a blanket of light. I was a seed planted in the desert that had a secret source of shade and water, which meant that I could grow."

I led my son in the prayer of salvation, and at the age of six Dan gave his life to follow Jesus.

We were able to help a lot of young people during those years. One day, though, when Dan was still just a baby, my husband said to me, "Linda, I have decided to once again use drugs and drink beer. Don't worry. It won't hurt anything." I was shocked and scared, more so now that I had a little baby to care for.

I was invited to Poland to preach and I took Dan with me. When I returned home, I couldn't find my husband. Then a friend told me the news. He had run off with another woman. I was broken hearted once again. This led to a divorce.

The Voice

CHAPTER THIRTY-SIX

RAISING MY SON

I was finally able to move out of Christiania into a nice little house, this time not as a missionary, but as a regular mother. The mistakes and misfortunes had taken their toll on me. Besides, I now had the responsibility of raising my only son. Therefore ministry in the traditional sense was put on the shelf. The long stretch of being in the midst of revival came to an end. Now I worked to make money as a regular mom to pay the bills and to be able to take good care of my boy. Though not in ministry as such, I lived a Christian life and taught my son to do the same. He was a boy of intelligence and excellence in whatever he did.

At the age of 12 Dan was baptized in the Holy Spirit, and at the age of 13 Dan entered into the ministry in our hometown. He told the local newspaper he was going to start up a teenage Gospel choir. They printed the story. He had a successful group of teens singing gospel.

Later, he had weekly Bible classes. The dining room table was full of teenagers with their Bibles and notebooks learning from teacher Dan. Mom Linda always made something fun to eat and tea for afterwards. The youth loved my pancakes!

Today Dan Hegelund is an internationally renowned minister of the gospel. Together with his lovely wife, Mary, they have been serving the Lord faithfully, not only in Scandinavia but also throughout ex-communist countries of Russia, Ukraine, Belarus, the Baltic Nations, and Poland, as well as Germany and the USA.

Dan and Mary are missionary pastors in a local Assemblies of God church in Post Falls, ID, where they also run an independent Christian elementary and high school named River Tech School.

Dan is perhaps most known for his music ministry, having produced albums, raised up gospel choirs, and performed in big musical events such as in the Presidential Palace of Kiev, before the Latvian government, at the Lithuanian march for Jesus, as an instructor at Copenhagen Gospel

Festival, and a participant in Battle of the Choirs (TV 4, Sweden).

Back in Europe, Dan served as a full-time employee at New Generation Church, based out of Riga, Latvia. During this time, Dan trained worship teams all across the ex-communistic countries and partook in a revival after the fall of the Berlin wall, which probably exceeds the Jesus Movement revival! It would make for a great story and book in itself.

The Voice

CHAPTER THIRTY-SEVEN

SCANDINAVIA

Another exciting story is how the Jesus People Movement swept Europe. It is an amazing thing to realize what actually happened. I, Linda Meissner, had been placed in Scandinavia, and after a period of time, had brought forth fruit again with hundreds of Scandinavian youth accepting Jesus and becoming his disciples.

From 1972–1974 I started multiple Jesus Houses in Stockholm, Gotherburg, Jonkoping, Orebro, Malmo, Copenhagen, Christiania, Odense, Aarhus, Roskilde, Oslo, Bergen, Trondheim, Tromso, Stavanger, Reykjavik and other cities.

In 1972, shortly after I arrived, Jim and Sue Palosaari brought a team of thirty of their best disciples from Milwaukee, Wisconsin to Europe. They first landed in Copenhagen, Denmark, then traveled through Sweden, new believers and new disciples growing everywhere they went. In 1973 William Lowery came with forty Jesus People called *Christ Is The Answer* to Gothenburg, Sweden, where they held tent revivals. After Sweden, Jim and also William both traveled with the gospel to Finland.

When the weather turned cold in Finland they traveled throughout the rest of Europe. Jim took his disciples and went to London, UK, where they created the rock musical, "Lonesome Stone," which opened at London's Rainbow Theater, and then toured Great Britain. There in England, Jim helped start what was for many years the largest Christian music festival in the world, "Greenbelt."

I know of other fellow soldiers, Adrian and Debbie Simila, who brought a team of Jesus People from the state of Washington to Sweden and Denmark. They pioneered a big work in Scandinavia with tents and buses and preaching on the streets and in the city parks. They even went on to Eastern Europe.

These are the Jesus People that I know of who were fruits of the Pacific Northwest revival, and who came to Scandinavia at the same time as I did, bringing the Jesus Revolution with them.

There were also others such as Duane Pederson from *Hollywood Free Press* together with Lonnie Frisbee from Southern California who flew to Stockholm, Sweden, telling their stories to Swedes about what God was doing in Jesus People California. Duane Pederson produced a European edition of the *Hollywood Free Press*.

Duane, Lonnie, Jim, Sue, William, Adrian, Debbie, and I were all working in Scandinavia during the same period of time. As a result there remains until this day great fruit of the Jesus People in Scandinavia.

For example, Ulf Christiansson, a famous musician from Gothenburg, Sweden, shared a powerful testimony of how he had been on drugs and was one of the city's lost sheep. I asked him how he came to be a Jesus Freak. He said, "One day some Jesus People from America came to Gothenburg and set up their witnessing teams in the city park. One of them told me about Jesus. I became a Jesus man overnight, thanks to them that came." Ulf Christiansson travels and sings all over Sweden and the world, and has started a church in Gothenburg.

Stefan Christiansen became a Jesus freak in Oslo, Norway. He started a Jesus Revolution there. They did exactly what the JPA did in Seattle, and have the same buttons, bumper stickers, and sayings. They have a Jesus Army that reaches different cities in Europe. I do not know which one of us won him to the Lord, but it is a sure thing one of us did. In Denmark there is a very strong Jesus Freak, Christian Heedegaard. Dan says that he is probably the most effective evangelist to come out of Denmark. Amazingly enough we have learned that he, too, has received a mandate to move to America. He is currently based out of Orlando, Florida. There are many other Christian ministries that are strong today because Jesus People came to Scandinavia. Every year there is a Jesus March in Stockholm, Sweden of 20,000 Christians (in 2010). The Jesus People were born and are not dead in Scandinavia!!

CHAPTER THIRTY-EIGHT

THE CALL

In 2011 Dan traveled to southern Sweden to direct a Gospel choir. Before the practice, he kept getting the same strong thoughts again and again. He decided to call me. "Hello, Mom. Do you remember what happened in 1972?"

I thought, and replied, "Linda Meissner arrived in Europe."

"That's right," he said. He continued, "Do you realize what year it is, this coming year?"

I replied, "Well, it will be 2012."

"Yes", said Dan, "and what is the significance of that?"

I thought, "It is 40 years between these two dates."

Dan continued, "Forty seems to appear several times in the Bible. It is interesting to note that Moses left Egypt running away as a guilty murderer. He remained in the wilderness 40 years tending sheep. Then when God heard the cry and groaning of the children of Israel, He decided to deliver them. Instead of him finding a brave young man, he remembered Moses out in that desert. He appeared to Moses in a burning bush. Moses took notice to the word of the LORD."

Dan continued, "The LORD said, "Moses, I have heard their cry, come and return to Egypt with my message." Though he had been an eloquent speaker when he was in the palace trained under Pharaoh, he now felt like he could not speak. God was merciful and sent Aaron to help him. God gave him the message and the mission that was to be accomplished. Mother, I think this message is for you. I can see you returning to America, after these 40 years of being in Europe. Do you know what the name of Moses' firstborn son was? It was Gershom: for he said, "I have been a stranger in a strange land." Mother, you have lived in Scandinavia for 40 years among a people who were not your own."

I could hardly breathe, but Dan had to go to choir practice and our conversation was cut short.

Then I remembered the prophetic words from Doug Parris, former JPA:

"Forty Years since the Revolution, and the JPA movement's execution. Forty years since Washington Hall fell. I still remember the old battle yell! Fear not, thou little one, for thou shalt be the forerun of that which will happen across the Earth, a great and new spiritual birth."

The LORD began speaking to me again in a fresh and unmistakable way saying, "Linda, you are to return to America. The Jesus People Army is not dead, she is merely sleeping. Jesus says unto her, "Arise."

CHAPTER THIRTY–NINE

BOOT CAMP

About two weeks after this, on the way home from one of the choir practices, Dan said, "I just can't seem to get rid of the word 'boot camp,' which comes to me again and again. It did that all day yesterday too."

Once again, I could not believe my ears. I nearly couldn't breathe. I invited Dan to step into my study for a minute. I went over to my desk and picked up the poem as I had recorded it in Seattle in 1968.

The Voice

I read it aloud:

"Now who hath a boot camp formed
Where miracles and trainings are performed?
Oh yes, we're in a time of war
A time the spirit of the anti-christ doth soar
Above, about, in and out
Oh how can there be any doubt
That the coming of the Lord draweth nigh
Why even now the earth doth groan and sigh

Hear their cry, Hear their cry
A hundred million heathen die
The church so slow against Satan's blow
Who doth know? Who doth know?
Arise, Awake, Behold the earthquake
Alarm, Alarm, Yet it doeth thee no harm
The Chimes the Chimes, The signs of the times

Which way? Which way? Work while it's day.
Behold, Behold, Be filled and be bold
At last, At last, All has come to pass
Rejoice, shout glory,, The fullness of redemption story
Behold the bridegroom cometh - go ye out to meet him
Yet empty handed would thou go
While thousands perish far below?
In sin, in strife, in pain, in woe
None of my love or my grace to know?

Oh the pain, the pain of death
The death that eternally separates from God
Because the road of indifference was trod

Awake-Arise-Shout, Preach and Sing
Tell the World of the soon coming King
Prepare, Prepare, Everywhere
His eternal glory to share
Hear among the fallen man
Gods great salvation plan

Which way? Which way? Would you ask again?
In full obedience clean- without sin
Now walk the plain path that is before thee
With the eyes of faith by which you now see
Fear not little one for thou shalt be the forerun
of that which shall happen across the earth
A great and new spiritual birth
For thou art now with child – conceive
And seek not those that thou should please
Obey, obey, the old-fashion' way
Until you see the break of day.
Day Star with healing in his wings
The loosened captive, how he sings.
Amazed, Amazed that should know
All these blessings he doth bestow."

(Linda Meissner, 1968).

I knew good and well what that word meant. It was an unfulfilled prophesy that I had received from the Lord back in 1968.

Now the Lord is saying that the time for its fulfillment has come. We will make that Boot Camp and train believers to "Go into all the world and preach the gospel to every creature." (Mark 16:15) Just as Jesus commanded, " But you shall receive power when the Holy Spirit has come upon you; and you shall be witnesses to Me in Jerusalem, and in all Judea and Samaria, and to the end of the earth." (Acts 1:8)

CHAPTER FORTY

THE VOICE

I have heard *The Voice*. I understand now, that I am to return to America and God will help me to raise up a new Jesus People Army. This army will include those who were used of God during the 1960s and '70s youth revival. It will include the new generation of youth, who will hear the voice of Jesus calling them to take up their cross and follow Him.

There will be an Exceeding Great Army! As it is prophesied in Ezekiel 37:1–9, which reads:

"The hand of the Lord came upon me and brought me out in the Spirit of the Lord, and set me down in the midst of the valley; and it *was* full of bones. 2 Then He caused me to pass by them all around, and behold, *there were* very many in the open valley; and indeed *they were* very dry. 3 And He said to me, "Son of man, can these bones live?" So I answered, "O Lord God, You know." 4 Again He said to me, "Prophesy to these bones, and say to them, 'O dry bones, hear the word of the Lord! 5 Thus says the Lord God to these bones: "Surely I will cause breath to enter into you, and you shall live. 6 I will put sinews on you and bring flesh upon you, cover you with skin and put breath in you; and you shall live. Then you shall know that I *am* the Lord." 7 So I prophesied as I was commanded; and as I prophesied, there was a noise, and suddenly a rattling; and the bones came together, bone to bone. 8 Indeed, as I looked, the sinews and the flesh came upon them, and the skin covered them over; but *there was* no breath in them. 9 Also He said to me, "Prophesy to the breath, prophesy, son of man, and say to the breath, 'Thus says the Lord God: "Come from the four winds, O breath, and breathe on these slain, that they may live." 10 So I prophesied as He commanded me, and breath came into them, and they lived, and stood upon their feet, an exceedingly great army."

This army will share the good news of the Gospel everywhere in their cities and towns. I am to establish a new Jesus Coffee House. This will be an evangelism tool for a youth revival.

If not now, when? If not us, who? The LORD has uttered His Voice before His army! As it is written in Joel 2:1–11, which reads:

"Blow the trumpet in Zion, And sound an alarm in My holy mountain! Let all the inhabitants of the land tremble; For the day of the Lord is coming, For it is at hand: **2** A day of darkness and gloominess, A day of clouds and thick darkness, Like the morning *clouds* spread over the mountains. A people *come,* great and strong, The like of whom has never been; Nor will there ever be any *such* after them, Even for many successive generations. **3** A fire devours before them, And behind them a flame burns; The land *is* like the Garden of Eden before them, And behind them a desolate wilderness; Surely nothing shall escape them. **4** Their appearance is like the appearance of horses; And like swift steeds, so they run. **5** With a noise like chariots Over mountaintops they leap, Like the noise of a flaming fire that devours the stubble, Like a strong people set in battle array. **6** Before them the people writhe in pain; All faces are drained of color. **7** They run like mighty men, They climb the wall like men of war; Every one marches in formation, And they do not break ranks.

8 They do not push one another; Every one marches in his own column. Though they lunge between the weapons, They are not cut down. **9** They run to and fro in the city, They run on the wall; They climb into the houses, They enter at the windows like a thief. **10** The earth quakes before them, The heavens tremble; The sun and moon grow dark, And the stars diminish their brightness. **11** The Lord gives voice before His army, For His camp is very great!..."

I will need many volunteers for this great work that God wants done. Will you please prayerfully consider what your role in this new work may be?

My son, Dan Hegelund, along with his wife, Mary, have volunteered to train worshippers to praise the Lord, and will form both a band and Gospel choirs to assist the new Jesus People Army that the Lord will raise up. There will be bands, busses, and banners. There will be every kind of talent needed to get the job done: Gospel singers, musicians, photographers, reporters, videographers, sound technicians, artists, intercessors, counselors, soul winners, marketing people, mechanics, cooks, willing cleaners, actors, speakers, to name a few.

They are all needed, both young and old. What does age have to do with it? God called Moses when he was 80 years old. Sarah gave birth when she was past her age at 90. And He's calling me now.

However, the primary goal and focus will be on the new generation from 13 to 30. So if you are a young person reading this story, this call is for you!

I was just 19 when God called me, an Iowa farm girl, to walk the streets of New York. Dan was just 13 when he started his first gospel choir and Bible studies in our home. So whether you are young or old, do not let this opportunity pass you by. God is calling young and old alike to take up their crosses and follow Him.

We will pass the torch with the Light of Jesus Christ on to the next generation. Together we can!

The Voice

SINNER'S PRAYER

If you have not met the Lord Jesus Christ yet then you can do so right now. You can use your own words or pray this simple prayer:

Father God
I come to you right now in the name of Jesus
I come to you just the way I am
I'm sorry for my sin, please forgive me
I open the door to my heart
and I ask you Jesus to come into my life
I believe in my heart and I confess with my mouth
that from this moment on you are my Lord and Savior
From this day on I will follow you
Thank you for saving me now
and making me a child of yours
I am saved
In Jesus name
Amen

The Voice

APPENDIX

UPDATE 2021

We have started an on fire, spirit-filled ministry in the Inland Northwest of Spokane, Post Falls, and Coeur d'Alene. We have a Jesus Coffee House, choirs, street evangelism, and street church. Jesus said, "Go into all the world," so we are making strategic plans to expand on the mission field in Vladivostok, Russia. Dan and Mary also started and oversee an independent Christian elementary and high school in Post Falls called River Tech School.

We have a big vision from the LORD, and we need helpers to carry our the mission. The harvest is great, but the laborers are few. Don't stand on the sidelines. Get in the fight. Take up the cross and follow Jesus.

Visit our website at www.faithc.org

THE MISSION

Our mandate and mission is threefold:

1. Raise Up a New Generation of Champions.
2. Rebuild the Lord's House.
3. Water the Valleys of the World.

Raise Up a New Generation of Champions

The Lord asked, Where are my champions? My Davids, Samsons, and Joshuas? My Esthers, Miriams, and Marys? The Lord has given us a mandate to raise up a new generation of champions. Here the story of Gideon's three hundred men of valor is an inspiration, as is the story of Ezekiel in the valley of dry bones. God asked Ezekiel, can these bones live? A big part of this mandate is our Courses & Classes available at www.faithc.org

Rebuild the Lord's House

Nehemiah's heart broke when he learned that Jerusalem
lie in ruins. He had heard that things were not good, but
it did not sink in until he saw the details for himself. He
looked at the gates and examined the walls, and found
it was in shambles. Today God is calling us to rebuild
the Lord's House, and the mandate comes with a
promise: The glory of the latter house will be greater
than the former.

Water the Valleys of the World.

The Garden of Eden had four rivers that watered the
surrounding dry lands. The Bible says, "A fountain
shall come forth from the House of the Lord and water
the Valley" (Joel 3:18). Wherever these rivers flow the
land is healed (Ezekiel 47:9, 12, Revelation 22:1-2, and
Isaiah 41:18, 43:19, and 44:3). The Lord wants rivers
of life to flow from our ministry in the Inland
Northwest and water the surrounding lands and
nations. For more information visit our website at
www.faithc.org

Will You Help Us?

It's time to take a stand. Merely *going* to church and *doing* church is tiresome and mundane. God is raising up an army of revivalists. We need your help. Come help us make a difference by taking the gospel to the world.

Reach out to Linda Meissner at **linda_may7@hotmail.com** or Pastor Dan at **dan@faith.org** and let us know when you are coming. You can also find me on social media at **www.facebook.com/linda/meissner.7**

Let the dead bury the dead, come now and be follower of Jesus.

GOD'S LOVE LETTER TO YOU

Love seems like a tiny drop falling inside the rushing sound of life's waterfall, as pain tries to overwhelm love with its noise and force. But love possesses one quality that pain does not. Eternity. Love can never be snuffed out by anything life throws at it; love has an eternal quality that can never be extinguished.

"God himself goes before you and will be with you; He will never leave you nor forsake you. Do not be afraid; do not be discouraged" (Deu 31:7).

When everything else has passed away; life, struggle, pain, illusions, and sorrows… one thing will remain. Underneath the rubble; underneath the many lies and shadows, one truth will remain: You are, you have always been, and you will always be loved.

"Where can I go from Your Spirit? Or where can I flee from Your presence? If I ascend into heaven, You are there; If I make my bed in hell, behold, You are there. If I take the wings of the morning, And dwell in the uttermost parts of the sea, Even there Your hand shall lead me, And Your right hand shall hold me. If I say, "Surely the darkness shall fall on me," Even the night shall be light about me; Indeed, the darkness shall not hide from You, But the night shines as the day; The darkness and the light are both alike to You." (Psalm 139:7-12) I can hear God calling out to you:

"Do not be afraid. Your darkness is as light to Me. Your pain is a fragrance of praise. Your tears I collect and wear as a necklace around My neck.

Even when you doubt me, when you curse me, when you deny me (though I am right there beside you holding you together).

Every beat of your heart, every breath you take, every move you make, overwhelms me with love for you.

If for but a split second you could see yourself as I see you, you would tremble at your own magnificence. Because you can't see yourself the way I see you, you are in so much pain.

Take My hand, hold Me near. All is well.

I am always near you. Reach out and touch me.
I... Love... YOU. I always have, I always will.
Nothing will ever change that."

Aren't you tired of quick fixes? God is looking for an
enduring relationship with you; an eternal life that is
nurtured and grows like a tree.

"For God so loved the world that he gave His one and
only Son, that whoever believes in Him shall not perish
but have eternal life" (John 3:16). The world can't
solve your problems. You don't need more self-help.
Jesus said "That which is born of flesh is flesh, but that
which is born of the Spirit is spirit... You must be born
again" (John 3:6-7). When your spirit comes alive and
God begins to live inside you, you can begin to live life
from the Spirit, and as a result your soul and body will
be restored.

You have lived for the world, now live for Jesus. He
died for you; will you live for Jesus?

www.ingramcontent.com/pod-product-compliance
Lightning Source LLC
Chambersburg PA
CBHW021230090426

42740CB00006B/462